Children's Services
in the
American
Public Library

Children's Services in the American Public Library

A Selected Bibliography

Compiled by
Fannette H. Thomas

Bibliographies and Indexes
in Library and Information Science, Number 4

GP

GREENWOOD PRESS
New York • Westport, Connecticut • London

Library of Congress Cataloging-in-Publication Data

Thomas, Fannette H. (Fannette Henrietta)
    Children's services in the American public library : a selected
bibliography / compiled by Fannette H. Thomas.
        p.   cm. — (Bibliographies and indexes in library and
information science, ISSN 0742-6879 ; no. 4)
    Includes indexes.
    ISBN 0-313-24721-8 (lib. bdg. : alk. paper)
    1. Libraries, Children's—United States—Bibliography.
2. Children—United States—Books and reading—Bibliography.
3. Children—Services for—United States—Bibliography.   4. Public
libraries—United States—Bibliography.   5. Library science—United
States—Bibliography.   I. Title.   II. Series.
Z718.2.U6T46   1990
027.62'5—dc20   90-40197

British Library Cataloguing in Publication Data is available.

Library of Congress Catalog Card Number: 90-40197
ISBN: 0-313-24721-8
ISSN: 0742-6879

First published in 1990

Greenwood Press, 88 Post Road West, Westport, CT 06881
An imprint of Greenwood Publishing Group, Inc.

Printed in the United States of America

∞

The paper used in this book complies with the
Permanent Paper Standard issued by the National
Information Standards Organization (Z39.48-1984).

10 9 8 7 6 5 4 3 2 1

This work is dedicated to
Joseph and Agnes Thomas

Contents

Preface

When the doors of the public libraries in America were opened, they were organized as institutions to serve the adult population of a community. Children were not considered a part of the public library's initial clientele. As early as 1876, there were professionals within librarianship who advocated the juvenile's right to use the public library. From that point onward the young began to attract attention as a potential core of library users, and they became the actual focus of a corps of professionals within public librarianship.

It was the goal of this work to study the whole configuration of children's services in the American public library through a bibliographic analysis of the professional literature of librarianship. Starting with the year of 1876 and continuing for a period of a hundred years to 1976, the professional literature was reviewed to reflect the major developments, trends, innovations, and practices that evolved or emerged in children's work. The result is this selected bibliography on children's services in the American public library: 1876-1976.

To codify the work, the study is classified by broad topics: (1) Historical focus, (2) Professional staff, (3) Organizational scheme, (4) Philosophical perspective, (5) Client group, (6) Collection development, (7) Readers' services, (8) Story hour, (9) Interagency cooperation, and (10) Multi-media. Under each topic the bibliographic entries are arranged in alphabetical order with each entry annotated. Through this bibliographic exploration the whole arena of children's services has been examined in terms of its evolution as well as the emergence of major developments, trends, innovations, and practices.

I wish to acknowledge the support in this project of the staff of the General Reference and Information Department at Enoch Pratt Free Library, Baltimore, Maryland. Thanks goes to the Public Services staff of the James A. Newpher Library at Essex Community College, Baltimore County, Maryland, especially Lenore Hash, Margaret Hurd, Darlene J. Little,

Nicholas Palmere, Carolyn Payton, William Presley, Geraldine Stipek and Joyce Wheeler. A special thank you goes to Joyce Middleton for all her efforts on the computer.

Introduction

In the annals of the American public library movement, children's services has been acclaimed as one of the great contributions of this social institution. In 1950, the Public Library Inquiry, the most comprehensive study yet done, concluded that "children's rooms and children's librarians have been the classic success of the public library."

The first work with children was done through the schools. In the 1880's, teachers' cards, baskets of books, and special lectures which were held in the library, were the methods used by the public libraries to serve children. The materials for children were culled from the adult collections. The early librarians who served children were adult librarians, such as Samuel Swett Green, Caroline M. Hewins, Lutie E. Stearns, Minerva Sanders, and others. Since the directors were the only professional librarians on staff in the early public libraries, they became the first advocates for service to the young.

As the doors to public libraries opened to children in the 1890's, books suited for them were slowly set aside. First, it was a shelf, then an alcove. Making their presence felt more, children were finally placed in rooms of their own. In Brookline (MA), Denver, Milwaukee, Brooklyn, Boston, Buffalo, Minneapolis, Pittsburgh, and in other urban centers the early children's rooms appeared. Here books and children were isolated, so as not to disturb adults. Despite the reasoning for separate children's rooms, they would become important facets of the service to children in the American public libraries.

Then came the pioneers in children's librarianship: Ann Carroll Moore, Clara W. Hunt, Mary Ella Dousman, Caroline Burnite, Effie L. Power, and Frances Jenkins Olcott, and Mary E. S. Root. With their appearance, a whole spectrum of services surfaced in the arena of public librarianship. In addition to providing reference services and readers' guidance for the young, other activities and methods such as reading clubs, the library league, home libraries, and

special lectures with book talks and lantern slides became
vehicles for stimulating interest in quality literature for
the young. Children's work, story hours, and reading aloud
became the most popular techniques used to provide groups of
children with good literature.

Ideas were shared and exchanged at ALA conferences where
children's librarians and their supporters gathered.
Articles continued to appear in the professional literature
about every facet of children's services. Manuals were
written or compiled to enlighten new librarians as well as to
share ideas with more seasoned professionals. Library
schools began to address this new specialty and major public
library systems developed training classes in children's
work.

As the professionals within children's librarianship
matured, book reviewing evolved on a more sophisticated
level. Anne Carroll Moore of the New York Public Library was
the leader on this front, following the path that was charted
by Caroline M. Hewins of the Hartford Public Library.

Through the professional literature can be traced the
developments in children's work as they surfaced in the arena
of public librarianship. On the pages of the professional
publications can be found the concerns of this segment of the
profession. Highlighted in the professional literature are
the changes in techniques that were used to serve children as
these methods responded to the new technologies. Even though
"outreach" to the communities that public libraries served
reached its peak in the 1960's, children's work has had a
tradition of outreach mode operative throughout its history.

Captured on these pages are the articles and books that
reflect the tenor of children's work in the American public
library. Herein are the techniques, services, and concerns
that have been manifested in children's services from 1876 to
1976 as recorded by professionals within children's
librarianship and of public librarianship.

Children's Services
in the
American
Public Library

1

Historical Focus

1.001   Batchelder, Mildred. "A Reflection on 27 Years of Librarians' Concerns for Children and Young People." Top of the News 27 (1971):156-176.

Using a dual format, a history of Top of the News was presented, along with a content analysis of the journal. Top of the News evolved from a newsletter by the Division of Libraries for Children and Young People. Volume one came out in October, 1942 and was still in a Newsletter format.

1.002   Brass, Linda J. Eighty Years of Service: A History of the Children's Department Seattle Public Library. Seattle, WA: Seattle Public Library, 1971.

Using 1891, as the starting date of children's services in the Seattle (WA) Public library, the history is traced to 1971. A little over four hundred books were placed on a shelf behind the circulation desk for children. In 1971, the children's department consisted of 300,000 books in two dozen outlets and had twenty-six librarians to serve children.

1.003   Broderick, Dorothy M. "Plus Ca Change: Classic Patterns in Public/School Library Relations." School Library Journal 14 (1967):31-33.

Starting with the year 1876, the author reviews the theory that governed public/school library relations. It was the public library reaching out to the schools as a co-educator.

1.004   Bush, Mildred. "Book Week Comes of Age." <u>Illinois</u>
         <u>Libraries</u> 21 (1939):29-32.

         In its twenty-first year, Children's Book Week had
         come of age. Over the years, many professionals and
         artists had contributed to the success of the
         celebration of children's books.

1.005   <u>Children's Library Yearbook</u>: <u>Number One</u>. Compiled
         by The Committee on Library Work With Children of
         the American Library Association. Chicago: American
         Library Association, 1929.

         This volume initiates a series of volumes on
         children's services. Covered in the volume are the
         administrative facets of the service, the personnel,
         the facilities, and juvenile books. A number of the
         articles address the international area in
         children's work. In Appendix IV, was the plan for a
         department of children's services at ALA's
         headquarters.

1.006   Cushman, Alice B. "A Nineteenth Century Plan for
         Reading: The American Sunday School Movement."
         <u>Horn Book</u> 33 (1957):61-71.

         This is a history of the American Sunday School
         Movement and of the materials which composed their
         libraries.

1.007   Eastman, Linda A. "The Library and the Children:
         An Account of the Children's Work in the Cleveland
         Public Library." <u>Library Journal</u> 23 (1898):142-144.

         Out of interagency cooperation with schools and
         branch libraries, grew the need for work with
         children in the Cleveland (OH) Public Library. In
         1897, the library opened a juvenile alcove in the
         main library, where all books for the young were
         housed.

1.008   Federici, Yolanda D. "Children's Services."
         <u>Illinois Libraries</u> 54 (1972):286-290.

         For the Chicago (IL) Public Library, children are an
         important element of its patrons. This presentation
         covers the history of children's services at the CPL
         and reflects the current scene.

1.009   Federici, Yolanda D. "History of Public Library
          Service to Children in Illinois." Illinois
          Libraries 50 (1968):962-970.

          This history of children's services in the state of
          Illinois is related with the national growth of
          children's work as parallel to the state scene.

1.010   Fenwick, Sara Innis. "Library Service to Children
          and Young People. Library Trends 25 (1976):329-360.

          The objective of this presentation was to trace the
          development of children's work in the American
          public library. Presented were the antecedents to
          children's services before 1876.

1.011   Filstrup, Jane Merrill. "THE ENCHANTED CRADLE:
          Early Storytelling in Boston." Horn Book 52
          (1976):601-610.

          Recounted is the history of children's work and
          storytelling in the Boston (MA) Public Library.
          Storytelling was launched at BPL when Marie Shedlock
          performed in the lecture hall of the central library
          in 1902. Sustained story hour programming did not
          start in BPL until 1910, when Mary W. Cronan,
          kindergarten teacher and storyteller, conducted a
          Friday afternoon program at the South End Branch.

1.012   Hanaway, Emily S. "The Children's Library in New
          York." Library Journal 12 (1887):185-186.

          While at a meeting of the National Association of
          Teachers, the idea was entertained to provide
          reading rooms for children in New York, NY. This
          article chronicles the development of that project.

1.013   Hewins, Caroline M. "Work With Children: What
          Libraries Have Done and Are Doing." Library Journal
          25 (1900):119-121.

          Tracing the development of children's work, Hewins
          cited the Sunday School library and the Young Men's
          Institutes as the precursors to public library work
          with children. Discussed are the personal
          requirements of the professional children's
          librarian.

1.014   Jackson, Clara O. "Service to Urban Children." In
          Sidney L. Jackson, Eleanor B. Herling & E. J.
          Josey's A Century of Service: Librarianship In The
          United States and Canada. Chicago: American
          Library Association, 1976. pp. 20-41.

          A review is made of the highlights in children's
          services in the public library from 1876 to the
          1970's.

1.015   Jordan, Alice M. "The Children's Place in the
          Library." More Books 2 (1927):273-276.

          When the Boston (MA) Public Library first opened, it
          was strictly an institution, which was designed for
          adults. It was not until the 1890's that a
          children's room was devised for the central library.

1.016   Long, Harriet G. Public Library Service to
          Children: Foundation and Development. Metuchen,
          NJ: The Scarecrow Press, Inc., 1969.

          Placing children's work in the mainstream of
          history, Long shows how it evolved in the public
          library. How children's work developed in the
          Cleveland (OH) Public Library serves as an example
          of children's librarianship in the public library.

1.017   Lopez, Manuel D. "Children's Libraries: Nineteen
          Century American Origins." The Journal of Library
          History 21 (1976):316-342.

          The historical precursors to children's work in the
          public library are discussed, such as the Sunday
          School Libraries and the School District Libraries.
          Caroline M. Hewins is cited for her early work with
          children. Cited also are Emily S. Hanaway of New
          York City and Charles Wesley Birtwell of Boston, MA.
          Then there follows the development of children's
          work within the arena of the public library.

1.018   Moore, Anne Carroll. "The Creation and Criticism of
          Children's Books: A Retrospect and a Forecast."
          ALA Bulletin 28 (1934):693-701.

          Starting with a historical focus, cited was the work
          of Horace E. Scudder, Mary Mapes Dodge, Miss Hewins,
          and the Sargents to bring quality to young readers.
          Then the arena for children's librarians within ALA
          was discussed. Presented were three simple canons

for selection: "1) Is the book alive? 2) Am I glad
it is alive? [and] 3) Why?"

1.019   Moore, Anne Carroll. "Touchstones for Children's
         Libraries." Bookman 63 (1926):579-586.

         Children were not numbered among the initial patrons
         of the library. As their presence was felt on the
         library scene, children were permitted in to
         separate quarters in the public library to segregate
         them from the adults. Other events in the chain of
         progress were presented to reflect how children
         became patrons of the public libraries.

1.020   Moulton, Priscilla L. "A Romance of The Round
         Table." Horn Book 44 (1968):289-296; 579-586.

         The Round Table convened on October 26, 1906 in the
         children room of the Boston (MA) Public Library. It
         was a gathering of the children's librarians in the
         greater Boston area, providing a platform for their
         professional concerns.

1.021   Overton, Jacqueline. "The Children's Library of
         Westbury: Its First Twenty-five Years." Horn Book
         25 (1949):451-466.

         On June 24, 1924, the children's library of
         Westbury, Long Island, New York opened. For twenty-
         five years, it had served as a site for education
         and culture in the area.

1.022   Plummer, Mary Wright. "The Work for Children in
         Free Libraries." Library Journal 32 (1897):679-686.

         According to this article, the first children's room
         was in the Public Library of Brookline, MA in 1890.
         When this study was completed a number of public
         libraries had children's rooms, but age limits, as
         well. Then the discussion covered the practices and
         ideas about this new public library service.

1.023   Power, Effie L. "A Century of Progress in Library
         Work with Children." Library Journal 58 (1933):822-
         825.

         Presented were the sites, the librarians, and the
         milestones in the development of children's work in

the public library. As early as 1876, librarians
acknowledged the need to serve children, if it was
to be considered an educational institution.

1.024   Rathbone, Josephine A. "Co-operation Between
          Libraries and Schools: An Historical Sketch."
          Library Journal 26 (1901):187-191.

          Serving as the germ for the development of library
          and school cooperation was the presentation of
          Francis Adams, who saw the need for the creation of
          a bridge between the public library and the school
          in the education of the young. Under the direction
          of Samuel S. Green, the Worcester (MA) Public
          Library devised the first program for school/library
          cooperation. Thus, the design was formed for a
          facet of librarianship that would become a component
          of children's work.

1.025   Root, Mary E. S. "An American Past in Children's
          Work." Library Journal 71 (1946):547-51; 1422-1424.

          Starting with the Bingham Library for Youth (1803),
          Root reminisced about the history of children's work
          in the library and on the national level, as well.
          She included her memories of her experiences with a
          young library movement in her youth.

1.026   Sasse, Margo. "The Children's Librarian in
          America." Library Journal 98 (1973):213-217.

          Over the years, the contributions of children's
          librarians have been greatly ignored in the
          professional realm of librarianship. The pioneering
          librarians abolished age limits, developed book
          collections, and established children's libraries to
          serve the young.

1.027   Sayers, Frances Clarke. "A Skimming of Memory."
          Horn Book 52 (1976):270-275.

          Recounted are the events that led Frances Clarke
          Sayers into children's librarianship. From
          Galveston, TX to the Carnegie Library School, Sayers
          made her way, until she met Ann Carroll Moore and
          was invited to the New York Public Library.

1.028   Smith, Elva S.   "The Carnegie Library School - A Bit
         of History." Library Journal 46 (1921):791-794.

         In October, 1900, the Carnegie Library of Pittsburgh
         organized a training class for five students in
         children's librarianship. Then in September, 1901,
         it formally launched the Training School for
         Children's Librarians. Herein is the history of
         that institution.

1.029   Spain, Frances Lander, Editor. "Reading Without
         Boundaries." New York Public Library Bulletin 60
         (November - December, 1956):631-640.

         These essays were presented to Anne Carroll Moore on
         the occasion of the 50th anniversary of the
         inauguration of children's work at the New York (NY)
         Public Library.

1.030   Sullivan, Peggy A.   "Library Service to Children:
         Celebration and Survival." Horn Book 52 (1976):262-
         269.

         Celebration has been a hallmark of children's
         librarianship, whether it is Children's Book Week or
         a special holiday. Survival of children's work is
         reflected in this article by the historical focus
         that has occurred in a hundred years of
         librarianship.

1.031   Sutherland, Suzanna. "Tomorrow's People:
         Children's Library Service in California."
         California Librarian 36 (April, 1975):10-29.

         To reflect the current picture, a historical
         overview of the school library, children's
         literature and children's work in the public library
         were presented. Outreach services and work with
         minorities are discussed. Working with the young
         establishes the foundation for the library of
         tomorrow.

2

Professional Staff

2.001   Akers, Nancy Meade. "Anne Carroll Moore: A Study of Her Work with Children's Libraries and Literature." MSLS Thesis, Pratt Institute Library School, 1951.

Serving as the first children's librarian of the Pratt Institute (Brooklyn, New York) Free Library, Anne Carroll Moore made many contributions to the development of children's librarianship in the American public library. In 1907, she became the Superintendent of Work with Children at the New York (NY) Public library, where she stayed for forty-five years, continuing her development of children's librarianship in all of its manifestations.

2.002   Andrews, Siri. <u>Caroline Burnite Walker</u>: <u>A Pioneer In Library Work With Children</u>. Cleveland, OH: Sturgis Printing Company, 1950.

What books and the library could do for the child as an individual and as a member of the community, was the justification for children's services in the public library. Through its book collection, the children's librarian, and its methods, the chief objective was to create a young reader who would become an adult user of the public library.

2.003   Baker, Augusta. "The Children's Librarian in a Changing Neighborhood." <u>Top of the News</u> 11 (March, 1955):40-41.

How the children's librarian responds to the new group among her clientele will be mirrored by the regular children in the community. The children's librarian needs to read books for adults on integration, join support groups, and review the

juvenile book collection for negative presentations
of minorities.

2.004   Baker, Augusta. "My Years As A Children's
Librarian" in The Black Librarian In America.
Edited by E. J. Josey. Metuchen, NJ: The Scarecrow
Press, Inc., 1970. pp. 117-123.

In 1937, Augusta Baker came to the 135th Street
Branch of the New York (NY) Public Library, where
she served as children's librarian for seventeen
years. Chief among her concerns was the publishing
of materials for Afro-American children.

2.005   Bechtel, Louise Seaman. "The Children's Librarian."
Library Journal 75 (1950):1774-1775; 1770-1796.

How astonished would the early pioneers in
children's work be to see what had happened in fifty
years of children's librarianship. The children's
librarian had untold influence on the juvenile
reading in the fifty's, but had competition from the
radio, television, and movies.

2.006   Bishop, Roberta. "Library Service to Children."
Library Journal 65 (1940):861-863.

Hoping to recruit others to library service for
children, the writer examined the work of a
children's librarian. Basic to the work of a
children's librarian were reference services,
cataloging, collection development, reader's
guidance, story-telling, and management.

2.007   Bostwick, Arthur E. "Library Work With Children."
ALA Bulletin 10 (1916):209-210.

Separate children's rooms, book collections, and
staff were very necessary for work with the young.
One critical comment was the lack of males serving
as children's librarians. One assistant in every
children's room should be male.

2.008   Bowker, R. R. "Some Children's Librarians."
Library Journal 46 (1921):787-790.

If early advocates could witness the work of
children's librarians now, they would have a sense
of pride in their accomplishments. Chronicled were

the achievements of Anne Carroll Moore, Clara
Whitehill Hunt, Effie Louise Power, Alice M. Jordan,
and Mary E. S. Root.

2.009   Broderick, Dorothy.   "Children's Librarians Are
        People."   Library Journal 86 (1961):1939-1941.

        To the questions: 1) Why are you a children's
        librarian; and 2) how come you wrote about adult
        books . . .; Broderick states that children's
        librarians are adults, too.

2.010   Broderick, Dorothy M.   "'Nothing' Librarians Cheat
        Children."   Top of the News 19 (December, 1962):26-
        27.

        Librarians who only concern was quiet in the library
        cheated children and youth of the opportunity of
        meeting good literature in their formative years.
        Books should be for hours to live; and the librarian
        played a keyrole in awakening the living that was
        found by reading books.

2.011   Burnite, Caroline.   "Instruction in Work with
        Children in Library Schools and Summer Schools."
        ALA Bulletin 3 (1909):420-427.

        Through a survey, information was ascertained on the
        status of professional training, which was being
        provided for those who were interested in children's
        work on the American scene.   It was the object of
        the study to foster a greater interest in the
        specialty and to create a ground swell for its
        support.   Responding to the inquiry were six library
        schools and eight summer schools.   What was being
        offered varied greatly in each situation.

2.012   Burr, Elizabeth and others.   "Wisconsin's Institute
        on 'Informal Learning Through Libraries.'"   Wisconsin
        Library Bulletin 51 (March - April, 1955):11-15.

        At an institute, which focused on adult education,
        the role of the children's librarians was explored.
        It was felt that the children's librarians had much
        to offer through their skills in reading guidance
        and group programs to the adult education movement.

2.013   Children's Library Yearbook: Number Two. Compiled
         by The Committee on Library Work With Children of
         the American Library Association. Chicago:
         American Library Association, 1930.

         The second volume in this series featured a number
         of articles for the professional children's
         librarian, a list of stories to tell and a list of
         adult books for youth. In the appendices were a
         directory of educational programs for children's
         librarianship and a directory of children's
         librarians, who were members of the American Library
         Association.

2.014   Children's Services Division: Preschool Services
         and Parent Education Committee and American
         Association of School Librarians: Early Childhood
         Education Committee (ad hoc). "Recruitment and
         Training of Volunteers to Work with Young Children
         and Library Materials." Top of the News 31
         (1974):63-67.

         By employment of volunteers, the library could
         expand its library services to young children. When
         an agency uses volunteers, they should have a good
         training program for the participants.

2.015   Comfort, Mildred Houghton. "Fare-Thee-Well,
         Downtown Book Lady!" Horn Book 37 (1961):468-471.

         This was a biographical sketch of Della Louise
         McGregor, who was the head of the Children's Room in
         St. Paul, MN. She retired on April Fool's Day in
         1961.

2.016   Corrigan, Adeline. "The Children's Librarian in the
         Community." ALA Bulletin 53 (1959):297-299.

         Discussed was the services of the Children's
         Department of the Cleveland (OH) Public Library.
         Stressed were the various ways children's librarians
         worked with all elements of the community.

2.017   Eastman, Linda. "The Children's Room and the
         Children's Librarian." Public Libraries 3
         (1898):417-420.

         In every public library, there should be a
         children's department or room or alcove. The
         children's room should be well-appointed. The

children's librarian should have a love for
children, a knowledge of juvenile books, an
introduction to library techniques, and an
understanding of the course of study in public
schools.

2.018   Ewing, Marion. "Working with Older Boys and Girls."
        Wilson Library Bulletin 10 (1935):244-249.

        For the children's librarian, there were some basic
        qualities that she should possess. She should have
        a genuine liking and respect for children,
        especially the individual. Her person and manner
        should be attractive. Lastly, she should have a
        high regard for good literature and the reading
        habit.

2.019   Fenwick, Sara Innis. "The Education of Librarians
        Working with Children in Public Libraries." MA
        Thesis, University of Chicago, 1951.

        The purpose of this study was to determine what
        should be the scope and content of the training for
        children's librarians in public libraries. To this
        was added an understanding of the objectives of work
        with children and what skills, as well as special
        knowledge were needed to meet these objectives.

2.020   Fitch, Viola K. "What Becomes of Children's
        Librarians?" Library Journal 76 (1951):162-163.

        This was an abstract that was taken from a thesis at
        Columbia University, New York, NY. Out in the arena
        of the public library, there was a shortage of
        children's librarians who transferred to other areas
        of librarianship because of pay and advancement in
        the profession.

2.021   Foster, William E. "Developing A Taste For Good
        Literature." Library Journal 22 (1897):245-251.

        Undergirding the development of an interest in
        quality literature in the young, should be the
        sharing of the personal enthusiasm for reading that
        was possessed by the librarian or the instructor.
        The effective educational mode in children's work
        was a cooperative responsibility of the schools and
        the public library, for each were conduits to great
        literature to which students should be exposed.

2.022   Glaberson, Bob. "Remembering Miss Berry." _Wilson_
         Library _Bulletin_ 35 (1960):314-315.

         A former juvenile patron pays tribute to the
         children's librarian of his youth. Not only is it a
         pleasant piece of reminiscence, it bespeaks of good
         librarianship.

2.023   Gold, Katharine E. "The Training Of Children's
         Librarians." _Public_ _Libraries_ 8 (1903):223-225.

         Conceding that professional training was important
         to the advancement of children's work. Gold found
         that there was a dearth of opportunity for study of
         it on the American scene. Although Pratt Institute
         had begun the first formal program in 1899, it was
         soon discontinued. By far the most complete
         professional program for training children's
         librarians was conducted by the Carnegie Library of
         Pittsburgh. Each training program incorporated
         practice work with the academic course of study.

2.024   Grady, Sister Mary Pauline. "What Makes a Good
         Children's Library?" _Illinois_ _Libraries_ 40
         (1958):151-152.

         The mark of a good children's librarian is her
         ability to motivate reading. Not only must she
         possess a knowledge of children's books, but she
         must have a love for children, as well.

2.025   Gray, Margaret. "Tricks of the Trade in Hawaii."
         Wilson _Library_ _Bulletin_ 34 (1959):259-263.

         A former children's librarian shares techniques that
         she employed to induce children to participate in
         class visits and story hours.

2.026   Green, Irene Smith. "Children's Work Means
         Happiness." _Library_ _Journal_ 74 (1949):626-628.

         In children's work, the most important factor is the
         children's librarian. Public libraries have the
         responsibility to pay children's librarians a good
         salary, to see that their jobs are not dead-end, and
         to offer positive moral support to the professional.

2.027   Hazeltine, Alice I.   "What Is A Children's
         Librarian?"   _Public Libraries_ 26 (1921):513-519.

         In response to the question: "Is the genus
         children's librarian becoming extinct. . .," the
         writer describes in detail the responsibilities of
         this professional. The children's librarian is
         responsible for understanding the young patron,
         interagency cooperation, collection development,
         readers' services, and storytelling.

2.028   Hewins, Caroline M. "Work With Children." _Public
         Libraries_ 10 (1905):475-476.

         During the formative years of children's work, the
         concepts, principles, and practices were shared and
         disseminated through professional meetings of all
         types. To such an end, Caroline M. Hewins held a
         series of meetings for interested professionals in
         the Connecticut area.

2.029   Hodges, Margaret. "A Laying On of Hands." _Catholic
         Library World_ 47 (1975):4-11.

         Discussed are four individuals - Elizabeth Nesbitt,
         Frances Clarke Sayers, Clifton Fadiman, and Virginia
         Haviland - who have had an impact on the development
         of children's librarianship. Their contributions
         will have impact on the future of children's work.

2.030   Hunt, Clara W. "Work With Children in the Small
         Library." _Library Journal_ 28 (1903):53-56.

         In a small library, the librarian had to be more
         mindful of the spending for books, which resulted in
         a greater interest in quality. Because there was
         usually not a separate children's room, the chief
         librarian interacted with all the patrons and
         offered more in-depth service.

2.031   Izard, Anne R. "Children's Librarians in 1970."
         American Libraries 2 (1971):973-976.

         In the 1970s, children's librarians were being
         declared extinct in their own time. This article
         addresses the need for children's work in the public
         libraries and the role of the children's librarian.

2.032   Izard, Anne. "The Children's Librarian - Public
         Relations Specialist." NYLA Bulletin 4 (August,
         1956):62-64.

         Through her work, the children's librarian is a
         public relations specialist. She works with
         parents, teachers, community leaders, and other
         professionals who work with children.

2.033   Kirk, Mildred E. "Displays for Recruiting
         Children's Librarians." Wilson Library Bulletin 32
         (1958):347-349.

         To stimulate interest in children's librarianship,
         the Cleveland (OH) Public Library designed a special
         recruitment display.

2.034   Latimer, Louise P. "Little Miss Merry and Other
         Fallacies." Library Journal 65 (1940):369-371.

         Giving children's work to a person who happened to
         like the young was one of the fallacies of
         librarianship. Children's work should be accorded
         the same respect, dignity, and salary as adult
         services.

2.035   Long, Harriet. "Children's Work: Part of Whole."
         Library Journal 74 (1949):858-859.

         At this time, there existed a need for children's
         librarians within the professional arena.
         Children's librarians played an important role in
         the realm of public librarianship because of their
         service to the community and to the young.

2.036   Long, Harriet G. "The Status of the Children's
         Librarian and Its Effect on Recruiting." Michigan
         Librarian 10 (June, 1944):3-7.

         There was a dearth of children's librarians in the
         profession. Among those who were in the service,
         many were leaving because of a lack of status, poor
         salary, and limited opportunity.

2.037   McIlvaine, Loretta. "The Young in Heart!" Wilson
         Library Bulletin 32 (1957):133-134; 136.

To answer the questions: Why are you a children's librarian; and what is children's work in a public library; a children's librarian gives reflections of her work day.

2.038   Mahony, Bertha. "Anne Carroll Moore - Doctor of Humane Letters." Horn Book 18 (1942):6-19.

This article was written after Anne Carroll Moore received an honorary degree from the University of Maine at Orono in June, 1940. Recapped is her career as a children's librarian, an administrator, a critic, and a writer.

2.039   Martignoni, Margaret E. "The Opportunity of the Children's Librarian to Serve in the Community." Catholic Library World 19 (1947):179-181.

Children's librarians enter the profession of librarianship as a permanent career. How can they in this capacity serve their community? They serve through the knowledge of the book collection, their educational background, their understanding of human nature, their social understanding, and their participation in the life of the community.

2.040   Martignoni, Margaret E. "Qualifications and Performance of Children's Librarians in Public Libraries of the United States." MS Thesis, Columbia University, 1951.

During the past few years, there was a shortage of librarians selecting the field of children's librarianship. To this end, this study investigated the academic and personal qualifications, as well as performance of children's librarians to ascertain the correlation between qualifications and performance.

2.041   Miller, Betty Davis. "Willye Dennis, Children's Services Librarian: 'The Hurts Don't Hurt Anymore.'" American Libraries 7 (1976):361-362.

Willye Dennis is the chief of children's service at Duval County Library System, Jacksonville, Florida. Before then, she was a children's librarian in the Duval System, where she reached out beyond the walls of the library.

2.042   Moore, Anne Carroll. "Ruth Sawyer, Story-teller."
         Horn Book 12 (1936):34-38.

         This is a biographical piece on the life of Ruth
         Sawyer, the great storyteller. In 1910, at
         Christmas time, she brought her special talents to
         the New York (NY) Public Library, where she was
         a part of their Christmas celebration for twenty-five
         years.

2.043   Moore, Anne Carroll. "Special Training For
         Children's Librarians. Library Journal 23
         (1898):80-82.

         When considering an individual for the position of
         children's librarian, attention should be given to
         her personal qualifications, her orientation to
         librarianship as a whole, and her training as a
         specialist within the profession. Her personal
         qualifications should be assessed through an
         introductory examination into a training program,
         while the focus of the training program would
         address the student's orientation to librarianship
         in general, as well as to the specialty within it.

2.044   Moore, Anne Carroll. "Training for the Work of a
         Children's Librarian." ALA Bulletin 8 (1914):238-
         243.

         Starting with a discussion of the program which was
         instituted at the New York (NY) Public Library for
         training children's librarians, there was a
         presentation of its composition. It was a six month
         session, including lectures, practicum, and a
         thesis.

2.045   Moore, Anne Carroll. "The Work of the Children's
         Librarian." Library Journal 28 (1903): 160-164.

         Stating the fact that the children's librarian's
         importance to the profession was reflected in the
         concept that she served as the medium between books
         and children. Because of this importance, the
         children's librarian should receive positive
         monetary compensation and good fringe benefits in
         her position; moreover, more professional regard
         should be demonstrated for this facet of
         librarianship.

2.046   Moreland, George B. "No Library Department is an
         Island: The County Unit." Library Journal 76
         (1951):1672-1675.

         In this time of crisis in children's work, there was
         a dearth of children's librarians coming into
         librarianship. Of the children's librarians who
         entered the field, many lifted the work for
         advancement and better salaries. The blame was
         placed on children's librarians, adult librarians
         and library management.

2.047   Nesbitt, Elizabeth. "Children's Libraries are Here
         to Stay - No Doubt!" Wilson Library Bulletin 26
         (1951):255-257.

         If the library is true to its educational purpose,
         then children's services is here to stay - no doubt!
         There exist a crying need for professionals training
         to be children's librarians in this period.

2.048   Nesbitt, Elizabeth & Harriet G. Long. "What Becomes
         of Children's Librarians and Why." Library Journal
         69 (1944):179-181.

         About 50% of the children's librarians were leaving
         this area of librarianship. The reasons for leaving
         were low salaries, moving into management, and for
         greater professional growth.

2.049   Olcott, Frances J. "The Pasadena Exhibit of Library
         Work With Children." Library Journal 36 (1911):345-
         347.

         An exhibit was designed by the Training School for
         Children's Librarians for the Pacific Coast and sent
         to Pasadena, CA. Using placards, photographs and
         printed matter, the exhibit aimed to show the
         various activities of a children's department and to
         explain the method used to reach children in a
         community.

2.050   Olcott, Frances Jenkins. "The Training of a
         Children's Librarian." ALA Bulletin 2 (1908):213-
         16.

         Drawing on a history of the Training School for
         Children's Librarians, therein was presented an
         overview of its work. A core of specially selected
         students were introduced to librarianship in a two

year program, which included both classroom work and
a practicum. The development of the course of study
started with the general in librarianship and moved
to the specifics of children's work.

2.051   Ostvold, Mildred R. "What's in a Name?" Wilson
         Library Bulletin 24 (1950):609-610.

         Using endearing terms to refer to children, should
         not be done by children's librarians. The
         children's librarian should make it a practice to
         refer to each young patron by his or her name.

2.052   Phinazee, Annette L. "The Early Childhood Library
         Specialist Program." Journal of Education for
         Librarianship. 16 (1976):183-188.

         In 1970, the School of Library Science at North
         Carolina Central University, Durham, started its
         program for the Early Childhood Library Specialists.
         The object was to provide for the learning
         experiences of children before they are six.

2.053   Power, Effie L. "Training for Library Work with
         Children." Library Journal 51 (1926):895-899.

         Every children's librarian should have: 1) a love
         of children, 2) knowledge of children's literature,
         3) knowledge of librarianship, 4) understanding of
         public instruction, and 5) the principles of
         psychology and education. To this end, a second
         year of study in library school was suggested.

2.054   Root, Mary E. S. "Charted Seas." Library Journal
         47 (1922):709-712.

         Speaking from her reminiscence, Root recalled the
         early librarians, who made a contribution to the
         beginning of children's work; and mentioned were her
         early reactions to children's librarianship.
         Training and recruitment of children's librarians
         were discussed.

2.055   Root, Mary E. S. "A Valiant Life - A Triumphant
         Death." Library Journal 51 (1926):1027-1028.

This was the professional obituary written for
Caroline M. Hewins, who died November 4, 1926.
Herein was given an account of her professional life
and her career from Boston (MA) to Hartford (CT).

2.056   Sasse, Margo. "Invisible Women: The Children's
Librarian In America." School Library Journal 19
(1973):21-25.

In the major biographical reference tools,
children's librarians are the invisible women and
are not included. Although considered the classic
success of American public libraries, children's
services has not been studied, nor have the
achievements of its founders been documented.

2.057   Sawyer, Ruth. "Anne Moore of Limerick, Maine:
Minister Without Portfolio." Horn Book 26
(1950):245-251.

In retirement, Anne Carroll Moore carried on her
crusade for quality literature for the young. Hers
was a full life, even though she was free from the
daily routine behind the library lions at the New
York (NY) Public Library.

2.058   Sayers, Frances Clark. Anne Carroll Moore. New
York: Atheneum, 1972.

This biography conveys the highlights of the life
and professional career of the grand lady of
children's librarianship.

2.059   Scott, Carrie E. "The Place of Library Work with
Children in the Training Class Curriculum." ALA
Bulletin 20 (1926):549-552.

Since the circulation of children's books
constituted one-half of the total, it figured in the
importance of children's work in a public library.
In a training class, at least, thirty hours of time
should be devoted to juvenile work. Covered should
be the administration of children's work, children's
literature, and storytelling.

2.060   Shaw, Spencer C. "Not What You Get, But What You
Give" in The Black Librarian in American. Edited by

E. J. Josey. Metuchen, NJ: The Scarecrow Press,
Inc., 1970. pp. 142-169.

Coming from a home where reading was a cherished
pursuit, Spencer C. Shaw was naturally attracted to
librarianship. He started his career as a branch
librarian, but enjoyed storytelling and children's
librarianship, which eventually followed as his
professional focus.

2.061   Smith, Faith E. "Library Work for Children."
        Public Libraries 12 (1907):79-83.

        What was the key facet for a successful program in
        children's work? First and foremost, it was
        considered the children's librarian, whose regard
        for children and their books was most important.

2.062   Tate, Binnie L. "The Role of the Children's
        Librarian in Serving the Disadvantage." Library
        Trends 20 (1971):392-404.

        According to Tate, all institutions in a community
        play a role in the child's learning process. It is
        up to these institutions to examine and reexamine
        how they influence the young.

2.063   Tate, Binnie. "Traffic on the Drawbridge" in The
        Black Librarian in America. Edited by E. J. Josey.
        Metuchen, NJ: The Scarecrow Press, Inc., 1970. pp.
        124-129.

        Binnie Tate likens libraries to castles of knowledge
        and states that it is the librarians challenge to
        build creative bridges to them. This she has done
        through children's librarianship.

2.064   "Training of Children's Librarians." Library
        Quarterly 5 (1935):164-188.

        The Professional Training Committee of the ALA
        Section for Library Work with Children made a
        preliminary study of the academic and professional
        courses necessary for a children's specialist in
        librarianship. Separate questionnaires were devised
        for children's librarians and managers of children's
        work. In both categories these were more than 50%
        replies.

2.065   "Training Children's Librarians of the Cleveland
         (Ohio) Public Library." Library Journal 41
         (1916):938-939.

         After functioning for three years, the Cleveland
         (Ohio) Public Library was able to state the
         rationale for maintaining its training program for
         children's librarians. To that date, thirty-three
         graduates had successfully completed the program and
         were gainfully employed by CPL and other
         institutions. Training its own corps of
         professionals had proven to be a cost effect
         endeavor for the library and its ongoing services.

2.066   "Training School for Children's Librarians at
         Carnegie Library, Pittsburgh." Public Libraries 11
         (1906):116-117.

         Out of its need for a trained corps of professional
         children's librarian, the Carnegie Library of
         Pittsburgh started a training school. Realizing
         that successful children's work in the public
         library was dependent on the quality of staff. It
         was a two year program that included the study of
         the whole spectrum of librarianship, as well as a
         strong component of practical application in its
         Children's Department.

2.067   Underhill, Ethel P. "Crumbs of Comfort to the
         Children's Librarian." Library Journal 35
         (1910):155-157.

         In spite of being colored by the prevailing
         mentality of the time, this article reflected how
         children's librarians ascertained the value of their
         work. Through personal feedback, this corps of
         professionals gleaned an assessment of the impact of
         children's work.

2.068   "What a Children's Librarian Should Know." Public
         Libraries 13 (1907):374-375.

         Stating that the experiences, the information, and
         the knowledge which a children's librarian should
         have was many and varied, this article produced a
         sample test. The test reflected personal concerns
         of the professional, exposure to a variety of
         persons, and the need to possess a positive reading
         habit.

2.069   Williams, Mabel. "Our Frontispiece: Anne Carroll
          Moore." Bulletin of Bibliography 18 (1946):221-223.

          Starting with her work as children's librarian at
          the Pratt Institute Free Library, Brooklyn, NY, Anne
          Carroll Moore gave forty-five years to
          librarianship. At the New York (NY) Public Library,
          ACM implemented a high standard of service and a
          continuing search for quality in children's books,
          especially through her reading list and review
          media.

2.070   Wright, Harriet S. "Miss Hewins and Her Class in
          Children's Reading." Library Journal 38 (1913):210-
          211.

          Sharing her wealth of knowledge in children's
          literature and services, Caroline M. Hewins of the
          Hartford (Connecticut) Public Library, held a
          special class for children's librarians in the
          Hartford vicinity. Conveyed through these sessions
          was the professional wisdom of one of the pioneers
          of children's work in the American public library.

3

Organizational Scheme

3.001   Bostwick, Arthur E.   "Volume of Children's Work in the United States."   <u>ALA</u> <u>Bulletin</u> 7 (1913):287-291.

Using a questionnaire, facts were gleaned about the status of children's work in fifty-one public libraries of varying size. The closing point of this study was the need for departmental status for children's services in the library's organizational scheme.

3.002   Crask, Catherine.   "An Art Library in a Junior Museum."   <u>Library</u> <u>Journal</u> 71 (1946):1170-1172.

In 1941, the Metropolitan Museum of Art opened a Junior Museum with a special library. The chief function was to interpret the collections to children, while the library in its correlation of books with museum objects and exhibitions helped to achieve this function.

3.003   Cutler, Marian.   "Developing a Children's Room." <u>Public</u> <u>Libraries</u> 19 (1914):242-245.

Since the physical make-up of a children's room was determined by its parent agency, the article focused on the book collection, the children's librarian, and the activities which were conducted therein. At the heart of children's work were the fundamental principles on which the work was based.

3.004   Dousman, Mary Ella.   "Children's Departments." <u>Library</u> <u>Journal</u> 21 (1896):406-408.

Discussed was the appointment of a children's room.
It was seen as an important component in the service
of the young by the public library. Then the
children's departments of the Buffalo (NY) Library,
Minneapolis (MN) Public Library, and Milwaukee (WI)
Public Library were highlighted.

3.005   Dana, John Cotton.   "Many-Sided Interest: How the
          Library Promotes It." The School Journal 73
          (1906):563-565.

          Although libraries were seen as bastions of
          scholarship, the public library was an operative for
          all citizens. To this end, the public library had
          the responsibility of informing the general public
          of its resources and of its services. Using the
          technological services of the day, the public
          library should actively court its patronage.

3.006   Farr, Harry. "Library Work With Children." Library
          Journal 36 (1911):166-171.

          Citing library work with children as the hallmark of
          the modern library profession, therein was presented
          its actualization on the American and British
          scenes. For both countries, the object of the work
          was to provide the young with positive reading
          matter. How children's work was conducted in the
          public library and in the school was addressed.

3.007   Field, Carolyn W.   "Library Service to Children" in
          The Library Reaches Out. Compiled and Edited by
          Kate Coplan and Edwin Castagna. Dobbs Ferry, N.Y.:
          Oceana Publications, Inc., 1965. pp. 105-134.

          Using children's work at the Free Library of
          Philadelphia as an example of effective children's
          librarianship, the writer discusses what composes
          children's services and the current scene.

3.008   Greenaway, Emerson. "No Library Department is an
          Island: The Surge Library." Library Journal 76
          (1951):1666-1672.

          Quoting the statement that children's work was the
          classic success of the public library, Greenaway
          discussed the reorganization of the Enoch Pratt Free
          Library (Baltimore, MD). Under this scheme the
          director of children's work became a coordinator of
          the work in the whole system, which was a staff

position. He even called for children's librarians
to join the Division of Public Libraries in the
American Library Association.

3.009   Gross, Elizabeth Henry. Children's Service in
         Public Libraries: Organization and Administration.
         Chicago: American Library Association, 1963.

         This study of the organization and administration of
         public library service to children in the United
         States was made in 1957-58. Included in the study
         were 1,000 libraries of varying sizes and in
         different locations.

3.010   Hall, Anna Gertrude. "Library Work with Children in
         Small Libraries." Wilson Library Bulletin 2
         (1923):131-134.

         What should be done for children in small libraries
         in villages and towns? In small libraries, there
         could be a successful program or scheme for work
         with children, and this article explained how such
         could be established.

3.011   Hunt, Clara Whitehill. Library Work With Children.
         Revised. Chicago: American Library Association,
         1924.

         This work was one of the resources in the A.L.A.
         Manuals of Library Economy series. Seen as
         essential to children's work were the librarian, the
         book collection and proper deportment of the young
         users in the library. A general overview was
         presented of the various techniques and devices,
         which were employed to stimulate the reading
         interest of children by librarians.

3.012   Jackson, Arabelle H. "Report on Library Work with
         Children." Library Journal 31 (1906):C89-97.

         At this ALA conference, services to distinct classes
         was being considered; and children form a distinct
         class within the public library. To ascertain the
         status of children's work in the public library a
         survey was sent to 100 of the largest cities in the
         U.S.

3.013   Jones, Virginia C. "The Plague of the Leprechaun."
         Wilson Library Bulletin 22 (1948):684-689.

Behind the creation and programming in the Anna Bird
Stewart Department for Young People was a resident
leprechaun, whose name was Shazy. When Ms. Jones
arrived in Paducah, Kentucky, there was no
children's department. She thought that the
situation was hopeless, but Shazy proved that it
could be a success.

3.014   Lucas, Mary Rinehart. The Organization and
         Administration of Library Service to Children.
         Chicago: American Library Association, 1941.

         Reviewing the organizational structure of children's
         services in twelve major public libraries, an
         assessment was made of the conceptionalization and
         the actualization of children's work as a formal
         construct in librarianship. Four administrative
         modes were identified for the operation of
         children's work, which were (1) advisory, (2)
         cooperative, (3) supervisory, and (4) control.

3.015   Maltby, Adelaide Bowles. "The Library's Work With
         Children." The Outlook 82 (1906):360-364.

         The children's department is the nursery of good
         citizenship. There are three elements which
         children's work should address, which are enrichment
         of life, greater knowledge, and the establishment of
         the reading habit. Discussed are the various facets
         of children's work.

3.016   Olcott, Francis J. "Rational Library Work with
         Children and the Preparation for It." Library
         Journal 30 (1903):71-75.

         According to this advocate of children's services,
         "national library work with children must adjust
         itself to the needs of the library as a whole, and
         be based on a study of the social conditions of the
         people who will use the library." It was incumbent
         on the children's librarian to know juvenile
         literature, as well as her community. Using the
         children's program at the Carnegie Library of
         Pittsburgh as an example, the work of that agency
         was the focus of discussion.

3.017   Olcott, Frances Jenkins. "Work with Children at the
         Carnegie Library of Pittsburgh." Library Journal 25
         (1900):166-168.

For the library, its chief goal was to impact on the lives of every child in Pittsburgh through the influence of good books. To this end, the best collection of literature was maintained under the supervision of an effective corps of professional children's librarians who employed a variety of techniques to foster reading, as well as worked with other agencies involved with children.

3.018   Ostvold, Mildred. "Accent on Children in the Branches." Minnesota Library Notes and News. 13 (September 1940):70-72.

To coordinate the work in branches and deposit stations, the position of Supervisor of Work with Children in Branches was created. The responsibilities for the position were contact with the outlets, school visits, story hour arrangements, collection development, and publicity.

3.019   Peterson, Harry N. "Administration of Children's Library Services." ALA Bulletin 53 (1959):293-296.

Using the organizational scheme of the District of Columbia Public Library as a frame of reference, Peterson discussed the administration of children's work. In considering the administration of children's work, the size of the community, the number of children, and the available funds are important factors.

3.020   "Reading Rooms for Children." Public Libraries 2 (1897):125-131.

Gleaned from a letter of inquiry was the status of children's rooms in American public libraries. Ten replies were received stating that a number of public libraries were providing areas for juvenile use which went from separate shelves to alcoves, then a separate room of their own.

3.021   Roos, Jean Carolyn. "Laying the Foundation." ALA BULLETIN 34 (1940):448-454, 490.

The foundation of library work was based upon services to children and youth. Fundamentally, all began with children's services, which was the cornerstone of public library services.

3.022   Scoggin, Margaret C. "The Nathan Straus Branch for
         Children and Young People." Library Journal 66
         (1941):547-549.

         The Nathan Straus Branch of NYPL was officially
         dedicated on April 30, 1941. The branch was
         completely devoted to work with children and young
         adults under the age of twenty-one. Contained
         therein was a discussion of the physical appointment
         of this facility.

3.023   Smith, Mary Rogers. "Los Angeles County Children's
         Work." Wilson Library Bulletin 29 (1954):163-166.

         How children's services is actualized in the Los
         Angeles (CA) County Public Library was the object of
         this article. This is the largest county in the
         world, covering 3,500 square miles. At the writing
         of the article more funds were extended for books
         and materials, then on personnel.

3.024   Smith, Mary Rogers. "Need More Children's
         Librarians?" Library Journal 87 (1962):811-813+.

         Discussed are the ways that the Los Angeles (CA)
         County Public Library met a shortage of children's
         librarians. Working through a systemwide and
         regional program, as well as projects, children's
         services is brought to the whole agency.

3.025   "Toward a Coordinated Program." ALA Bulletin 35
         (1941):574-579.

         In 1932, the Executive Board of ALA created a
         special board to strengthen the general phases of
         library services to youth - school, children's and
         young adults. Out of this board grew the Division
         of Libraries for Children and Young People, with
         staff at the ALA Headquarters. This was a summary
         report of the Board's activities from 1932-1941.

3.026   Van Kirk, K. "For Children - and No One Else!"
         American Home 25 (April, 1941):42-44.

         For children, most libraries were grim. In Palo
         Alto, California, there was open a delightful branch
         for children only. Presented was a description of
         the branch and the activities therein.

3.027   Van Norman, C. Elta. "Atmosphere in the Children's
        Library." Wilson Library Bulletin 10 (1936):382-
        385.

        Having a comfortable children's room where children
        felt at home, was of value to work with children.
        Color on walls, furniture, and throughout the room
        was important. Casual seating helped young folk
        relax and browse.

3.028   Vitz, Carl. "Standardization in Work with
        Children." Library Journal 53 (1928):805-808.

        To standardize children's work, libraries were
        organized into departments, which were both positive
        and negative. In the children's department, the
        young had access to a quality collection and the aid
        of the children's specialist. Yet, the young did
        not have direct access to the adult collection,
        which was necessary for their growth.

3.029   Warncke, Ruth. "Library Services to Children in the
        Mosaic of Administration." ALA Bulletin 61
        (1967):1324-1327.

        What the relationship between library service to
        children and administration maybe depends entirely
        on the goals of the institution. How direct the
        contact with children to the institution will be the
        key to administrative attention.

3.030   Weir, Sandra, Editor. "Administration of Children's
        Service." Illinois Libraries 57 (1975):1-62.

        Over the years, children's librarians have paid
        little attention to administration. However, with
        the negative turn of the tide, administration is
        assuming more importance in children's
        librarianship.

3.031   Wellman, Harold O. "Roof Reading - Rooms in the
        Branches of the New York Public Library." Library
        Journal 35 (1910):259-260.

        In June, 1905, the New York (NY) Public Library
        opened its first rooftop reading - room in the
        Rivington Street Branch. Not only the appointment
        of such a facility was discussed, but the use, as
        well.

3.032   Wheeler, Sara H.   "Children's Library Service in
        Minnesota." <u>Minnesota</u> <u>Library</u> <u>Notes</u> <u>and</u> <u>News</u>.   13
        (June, 1942):299-304.

        In 1941, a survey was executed in Minnesota
        communities of 5,000-30,000 with public libraries.
        The goal was to evaluate the level of children's
        services rendered in each community. Lacking in
        most communities was a trained children's librarian.

4

Philosophical Perspective

4.001   Andrews, Siri M. "The Future of Library Work with
         Children" A Symposium, Part V." <u>Library</u> <u>Journal</u> 62
         (1937):17-19.

         Training and the person who served as the children's
         librarian were fundamental to children's
         librarianship. Library schools needed to take a
         more positive stance with regard to the importance
         of children's librarianship. Established should be
         standards to govern professionals who functioned as
         children's librarians.

4.002   Babney, Elfrieda. "Beware - the Parents." <u>Wilson</u>
         <u>Library</u> <u>Bulletin</u> 15 (1940):232-233.

         There was not much a librarian could do about
         parents, who were a problem. In this category, fall
         parents, who want books to have values, who want
         their children to read things that they had, or who
         saw fines as negative.

4.003   Backer, Mary Askew. "Blueprint for Discipline."
         <u>Wilson</u> <u>Library</u> <u>Bulletin</u> 22 (1947):46-48.

         Although libraries were quiet, there are times when
         there were discipline problems. Handling discipline
         through a policy of prevention or calling the police
         were suggested. Under all circumstances, the
         librarian should maintain a sense of control of the
         situation, as well as, herself.

4.004   Bean, M. A. "The Evil of Unlimited Freedom in the
         Use of Juvenile Fiction." <u>Library</u> <u>Journal</u> 4
         (1879):341-343.

Public libraries provided unlimited access to
juvenile fiction. Reading a book of fiction daily
made students inattentive and cultivated a dislike
for studying.

4.005   Beem, Vilda P. "Guiding to Books." Illinois
         Libraries 7 (1925):129-131.

         To guide children to books required patience,
         kindness, sympathy and interest. The key to
         guidance was the development of a common "interest"
         on the part of the librarian with the child's.

4.006   Blinn, Marjeanne Jensen, compiler. Summoned by
         Books. New York: The Viking Press, 1965.

         Herein are essays and speeches by Frances Clarke
         Sayers. The topics cover librarianship as a
         profession, children's reading, professional
         personalities, storytelling and writing for
         children.

4.007   Bostwick, Arthur E. The American Public Library.
         New York: D. Appleton and Company, 1929.

         In this work which assessed the whole spectrum of
         public librarianship, children's services was cited
         as one of the modern developments on the
         professional scene. Discussed were the historical
         perspective, the practices then in vogue, and the
         rationale for, as well as against children's work in
         the public library.

4.008   Bostwick, Arthur E. "The Library and the Child."
         ALA Bulletin 20 (1926):281-287.

         In library work, children were a variable quantity,
         which had to be dealt with in terms of the
         individual, as well as a group. Children's work was
         one of the positive factors that had evolved on the
         scene in librarianship.

4.009   Bowerman, George F. "The Children's Department:
         Fundamental for Successful Public Library Work."
         Library Journal 65 (1940):953-956.

         Responding to the debate of placing all children's
         services in the school, this writer saw children's

departments as fundamental to the public library. As an educational agent, the public library had a commitment to serve juveniles.

4.010   Bowerman, George F. "Library Advertising." Public Libraries 10 (1905):335-339.

Libraries should glean lessons from commercial advertisers. Through its services, the building, and various media, the public library should advertise itself.

4.011   Bowerman, George F. "Library Work for Children." Wilson Library Bulletin 10 (1935):105-109.

Viewing the public library as a factor in education, the writer stated that the real purpose of education was for the achievement of adulthood. If the young learned the joy and benefit of voluntary reading through the library, the seeds were planted for life-long learning.

4.012   Breed, Clara E. "Ten Years Old." Wilson Library Bulletin 14 (1940):746-748.

After ten years in the profession, a children's librarian spoke out on what was positive and what was negative about her career. On the negative side were the salaries and the status of librarianship as a profession. Working with patrons and books were the positive aspects.

4.013   Broderick, Dorothy M. An Introduction to Children's Work in Public Libraries. New York: The H. W. Wilson Company, 1965.

In the first part of this work, the philosophy of children's work is presented, along with principles of book selection, management of a children's room and programming. The final section could serve as a collection development device.

4.014   Broderick, Dorothy. "A Pox on Both Their Houses." School Library Journal 18 (1971):92-93.

The New York state's Report of the Commissioner of Education's Committee on Library Development recommended that all library service to children be

placed in the school. This article assesses the
weakness of the public library and the schools,
stating a need for both.

4.015   Broderick, Dorothy. "Toward a New Formula."
         Library Journal 89 (1964):4972-4975.

         The pioneers of children's work left a firm
         foundation of principles on which the service is
         based. The principles should not change but the
         method's should change - every year.

4.016   Buell, H. C. "The Library and its Functions."
         Wisconsin Library Bulletin 3 (1907):17-21.

         Having a good book collection and an imposing
         building did not constitute an effective library.
         Central to the work of a good public library was the
         quality of its professional staff. At the core of
         the library's functions was the educational factor
         of its purpose and mission, which should be
         addressed through its programs and services.

4.017   Burke, J. G. "Where Will All the Children Go?"
         American Libraries 2 (1971):56-61.

         From the New York state's Report of the Commissioner
         of Education's Committee on Library Development 1970
         came the recommendation that all library services to
         children be placed in the elementary school media
         centers. Out of it arose a controversy over its
         recommendation. Presented herein are the major
         views in the controversy.

4.018   Burnite, Caroline. "Library Work with Children in
         War Time." ALA Bulletin 12 (1918):95-98.

         Because the war marked the close of one era and the
         beginning of another, children had to be
         resocialized. At the heart of this changing period
         was a new sense of patriotism, which was found in
         service and through reading.

4.019   Burnite, Caroline. "Values in Library Work with
         Children - II." ALA Bulletin 7 (1913):282-287.

Through children's services, children should be
introduced to books and materials that expand their
horizons and elevate their living. Influencing the
quality of reading matter which juveniles
encountered was the value of children's work. How
one system, the Cleveland (OH) Public Library
addressed this concern was discussed.

4.020   Burr, Elizabeth, and others.   "Are Children's
           Librarians Adult Educators?"   Top of the News 11
           (March, 1955):42-44.

           In response to the questions, a group of
           professionals attempt an answer. Children's
           librarians through their outreach services to the
           adult community do serve as educators of that
           segment of the population.

4.021   Burr, Elizabeth.   "Children's Reading - A Family
           Affair."   Wisconsin Library Bulletin 42 (1946):117-
           119.

           Stating a case for making reading a family affair,
           Burr stressed the importance of the home in the
           development of the reading habit. Predicated was
           the assumption that the home provided the
           fundamental basis for creating the child's
           orientation for living.

4.022   Burt, Mary E.   "The Muses in the Common School."
           Atlantic Monthly 67 (1891):531-537.

           When teaching young children reading, the use of
           classical literature would prove more valuable and
           enhancing, then the utilization of material found in
           required beginning readers. The classical
           literature not only offered a breath of language,
           but an expansive array of content.

4.023   Burt, Mary E.   "On Teaching Children to Read."   New
           England Magazine 1 (1889):426-429.

           The writer differed with the instructional process
           for reading. Usually, the instruction focused on
           the acquisition of a skill, while neglecting the
           higher principles which should be a part of the
           learning process.

4.024   Bush, Mildred. "The Children's Library - Its
        Opportunities and its Obligations." Illinois
        Libraries 9 (1927):80-85.

        Building on the foundation of education, the library
        became an institution for continued growth of the
        individual. If this ideal was established in
        childhood, there would be no need for adult
        education.

4.025   Butler, Helen L. "For Childhood's Inner Fortess."
        ALA Bulletin 36 (1942):175-178; 195.

        "Books, not bullets, [were] the reinforcements for
        the children's battlefront." In books, the children
        found a sense of security, the democratic ideals,
        respect for other cultures, as well as the practical
        realities of a world at war.

4.026   Carson, Jessie M. "The Children's Share in a Public
        Library." Library Journal 37 (1912):251-256.

        When public libraries first opened, children were
        excluded. Through the concern of teachers, children
        were slowly included in the patronage of the public
        library as it recognized its educational value.

4.027   Case, Gladys S. "Traffic Signals for the Children's
        Librarian." Public Libraries 30 (1920):470-475.

        For the children's librarian one of the goals was to
        instill an appreciation of reading outside of the
        school. It was an ideal that the children's
        librarian brought to her work through love of books
        and children.

4.028   Cecil, Sister. "Children's Reading." Catholic
        Library World 5 (1934):71-73.

        Important in this century was the rediscovery of
        childhood. In childhood, it was the mother, the
        teacher, and the librarian who were important
        factors in the reading process, with the teacher
        serving as the linking bond between home and the
        public library.

4.029   Chambers, Ruth Enke. "The Fun of Reading Aloud."
        Horn Book 24 (1948):177-80.

Sharing books with children through reading aloud
was a joy that adults should savor. It was a
positive activity for a family group and for
developing a love of quality literature.

4.030   Cheatham, Bertha. "Recapping a Restive Year." News
         Roundup '74." Library Journal 99 (1974):3237-3240.

         Presented are the newsworthy items and trends for
         1974 that had impact on children's librarianship.

4.031   Cheatham, Bertha. "SLT News Roundup" Library
         Journal 98 (1973):3669-3674.

         A review of 1973 is made to assess the newsworthy
         items and trends that are impacting on children's
         librarianship.

4.032   "Child-Concerned World." Wilson Library Bulletin 42
         (1967):165-205.

         America is a child-concerned country. To this end
         this issue addresses the professional concerns with
         children and youth.

4.033   Children's Library Yearbook: Number Three.
         Compiled by The Committee on Library Work with
         Children of the American Library Association.
         Chicago: American Library Association, 1931.

         This volume was developed with four sections on
         children's services: 1) juvenile books, 2) the
         arena of children's work, 3) trends in children's
         reading and 4) the European book market. Discussed
         was the work of the children's library at the
         Gillette State Hospital for Crippled Children in St.
         Paul, Minnesota.

4.034   "Children's Services" Illinois Libraries.   58
         (1976):783-828.

         Children's librarians have broken the mental and
         physical barriers of "basement status." Not only do
         children's librarians program for the young, they
         are concerned with projects that reach parents and
         other adults, who work with children. "Moving up"
         has become a motto for librarians. Move up from the
         basement and down from the ivory tower.

4.035   Colwell, E. H. "Children's Libraries." New Era 22
         (March, 1941):62-64.

         It should be the rightful heritage of every child to
         have access to a public library and its services.
         Serving as the key to service was the librarian.
         The other facets to effect children's libraries were
         a good book collection and comfortable physical
         facilities.

4.036   Dana, John Cotton. A Library Primer. Chicago:
         Library Bureau, 1899.

         The Library Primer was a manual designed for small
         libraries. In it were items that related to
         children's work, such as the library department of
         the N.E.A., young people and the school, assisting
         the school, the children's room, classroom
         collections, and home libraries for children.

4.037   Davidson, Letha M. "The Future of Library Work with
         Children: A Symposium, Part X." Library Journal 62
         (1937):285.

         In the future, children's librarianship would be
         shaped by the needs of juveniles, which it served.
         To this would be added, the interest of the parents
         and the school. Children's work would have an
         interesting future, if it maintained its ideals, and
         its methods were adaptable.

4.038   De Ronde Edie, Priscilla. "How the Library Meets
         the Children." Library Journal 65 (1940):97-100.

         Using the public library was a voluntary choice that
         children made. The fact that they came in such
         numbers was proof that children's work served a
         special purpose.

4.039   Dousman, Mary E. "Children's Librarians' Section."
         ALA Bulletin 2 (1908):372-382.

         During the first session at the Annual Conference,
         Anne Carroll Moore opened with a paper on "Library
         Membership as a Civic Force." Dr. Graham Taylor
         discussed "The Civic Value of Library Work with
         Children." At the second session of the division,
         presentations were made on old children's books and
         the value of folklore in education.

4.040   Eastman, Linda A.   "The Children's Room and The
        Children's Librarian." Public Libraries 3
        (1898):417-420.

        When children's librarianship was a novel entity on
        the professional scene, Eastman presented some of
        the fundamental concepts of the service. Described
        were the design of ideal quarters, the housing of
        the collection and the requirements for a specialist
        in children's work.

4.041   Edwin, Natalie.   "Standards for Children's Service.'
        California Librarian 19 (October, 1958):228-230;
        262.

        This was a working draft of the "standards" for
        children's service. It covered objectives,
        administration, materials, personnel, physical
        facilities and services to children.

4.042   Ely, Mary.   "Our Present Problem." ALA Bulletin 8
        (1914):219-223.

        Fostering the reading of quality literature was an
        objective of children's work in the public library.
        This objective was undermined by what books were
        being sold in bookstores and purchased for home
        libraries by adults.

4.043   English, Gladys.   "The Future of Work with Children:
        A Symposium, Part VIII." Library Journal 62
        (1937):114-115.

        It was the responsibility of the children's
        librarians to impart the importance of children's
        librarianship to management. At the state level,
        there needed to be divisions of children's work in
        the state associations.

4.044   Erskine, John.   "Reading for Young People." New
        York Libraries 3 (1912):39-43.

        Coming from the perspective of an advocate for
        "freedom of choice," the writer felt that a passion
        for reading was an individual option. Professionals
        were encouraged to respect always the point of view
        of the reader. Reading should serve as a stimulant
        for the imagination in the individual. Nor did the
        writer believe that fine novels and adventure

stories were negative factors on the reading
spectrum.

4.045   Field, Carolyn. "Sacred Cows: The CCLD Report."
          Library Journal 96 (1971):3445-3447.

          Children's work has been called the success story of
          the public library in the 20th century. If
          children's work is turned over to the schools, can
          the schools meet all of the needs of juvenile
          patrons of the library?

4.046   Foster, William E. "What Our Pupils Read Outside of
          School." Journal of Education 38 (1893):347-348.

          Creating an adult readership should be the objective
          of training and education in childhood. The public
          library and the school in concert should overcome
          the influences of the home and of peers in
          cultivating a positive reading mode in the young.

4.047   Gerhardt, Lillian N. "Public Library Services to
          Children and YA's: An Auto-Interview." Library
          Journal 101 (1976):109-111.

          Predicting the future for children's services,
          Gerhardt sees the schools assuming more
          responsibility for children's work. As the economy
          fails, there is a reduction in services to minors in
          the public library, especially in large urban
          centers.

4.048   Getzels, J. W. "The Child in the Changing Society:
          Implications for the Librarian." Library Quarterly
          27 (1957):267-278.

          This article addressed three questions. 1) What is
          the nature of the dominant American values? 2) What
          is the nature of the current cleavages and
          transformations in these values? 3) What are their
          effect on the child and what are the implications of
          this for the child's relationship to the library?

4.049   Greenaway, Emerson. "What About Tomorrow's
          Children?" Library Journal 75 (1950):656-659.

Opening and closing with a series of questions,
Greenaway wonders whose responsibility will
children's work be in the future. Will children's
services be the domain of the public library or the
school or the responsibility of both.

4.050   Greenberg, Marilyn W. and Ryna H. Rothberg.   "Don't
Underrate Service to Children." California
Librarian 37 (April, 1976):51-54.

Two professionals in children's librarianship,
review the strong points that make children's
service a viable facet of the public library.

4.051   Gross, Elizabeth H. "The Child and the Public
Library." ALA Bulletin 53 (1959):287-288.

As early as 1876, W. I. Fletcher voiced a concern of
the public libraries responsibility for children.
Since that time, the public library has demonstrated
its concern for services to children and their
importance as patrons. This concern is in keeping
with our national spirit of childhood.

4.052   Hall, G. Stanley. "Children's Reading: As a Factor
in Their Education." Library Journal 33 (1908):123-
128.

Did juvenile reading become a negative factor in the
child's education? There were times when children
should be learning from the practical side of life
that they miss because they are employed in the
exercise of reading. Carrying the discussion
further, the reading interests of boys and girls
were analyzed. In closing, there was stressed the
need for more storytelling.

4.053   Hazeltine, Alice I. "The Future of Library Work
with Children: Part IV." Library Journal 61
(1936):922-923.

After forty years, children's librarianship had
arrived at its middle age period, which was a time
for review of objectives and methods. Although a
sound principle - "the right book for the right
child," it needed to be addressed by research in the
profession and outside of librarianship.

4.054   Hazeltine, Alice I, Editor. Library Work with
        Children. New York: The H. W. Wilson Company,
        1917.

        This was the second volume in the series of Classics
        of American Librarianship. It included reprints of
        papers and addresses on children librarianship which
        were historical in nature. Opening this compendium
        on children's service was William Isaac Fletcher's
        "Public Libraries and the Young."

4.055   Henne, Frances. "The Basic Need in Library Service
        for Youth." Library Quarterly 25 (1955):37-46.

        According to Henne, the trends in library service
        for the young were the expansion of facilities,
        reiteration of goals and objectives, and extension
        of library services. The chief objective has been
        the reaching of all youth with good library
        services. Still many children were without service.
        Most important of all developments was giving youth
        access to libraries in their elementary schools.

4.056   Henne, Frances, Alice Brooks and Ruth Ersted.
        Youth, Communication and Libraries. Chicago:
        American Library Association, 1949.

        The articles were papers which were presented at the
        Library Institute at the University of Chicago,
        August 11-16, 1947. Stressed during the institute
        were 1) developments in education and communications
        that impact on library service to youth, 2) the use
        and analysis of communication media, 3) new concepts
        about the library as an agent of communications, and
        4) reports of new developments in librarianship for
        youth.

4.057   Hoyt, Franklin S. "Problems in the Production of
        Books for Children, with Special Reference to Some
        Wider Needs." ALA Bulletin 13 (1919): 282-285.

        Presented was the perspective of the publisher.
        Children should have a more global viewpoint in a
        changing world. The time tested technique of
        reading aloud should be utilized in the home and the
        library to keep quality literature before the young.

4.058   Hunt Clara Whitehill. "The Children's Library A
        Moral Force." Library Journal 31 (1906):97-103.

All education should be a moral force in the
development of the young. Through books, the public
library helps to mold and shape the boys and girls
for their responsibilities as adults and to be
positive citizens in adulthood.

4.059   Hunt, Clara W.   "Picture Work is Children's
          Libraries." Library Journal 25 (1900):66-67.

          Not all professionals supported the use of picture
          bulletins, which were used to attract juveniles to
          non-fiction. To prepare, the picture bulletin
          consumed a great deal of the children's librarian's
          time, which was an expenditure of money.

4.060   Hunt, Clara W.   "Values in Library Work with
          Children - I." ALA Bulletin 7 (1913):275-282.

          The value of children's work was directly related to
          the improvement in the caliber of reading matter, to
          which the young were being exposed. For children's
          librarians there was an ongoing need to campaign
          against some of the prevailing ideas of the time
          that pandered to the negative.

4.061   Hunt, Clara Whitehill.   "Work with Children in the
          Small Library." Library Journal 28 (1903):53-56.

          Seeing your situation through the eyes of another,
          can help create an appreciation for it - the small
          library. The chief joy of a small library is the
          interpersonal relationship that evolves between the
          librarian and the children.

4.062   Kerr, Willis H.   "The Child in the School and in the
          Library." ALA Bulletin 9 (1915):144-147.

          The child was the constant factor in all educational
          agencies, whether school, library, playground,
          church, or home. Although library work dealt with
          the cultural, it was a necessary part of education.

4.063   Ladley, Winifred C.   "Current Trends in Public
          Library Service to Children." Library Trends 12
          (1963):3-118.

A survey is made of the whole realm of children's
work from the historical background to a discussion
of all its manifest facets.

4.064   Latimer, Louise P.   "The Future of Library Work with
         Children: A Symposium, Part I.: Library Journal 61
         (1936):817-819.

         Opening with statements on the decline of children's
         work, Latimer saw the depression as a negative
         factor. Securing children's librarianship required
         good professional staff, effective selection of
         books, collection maintenance, and a positive
         atmosphere in the children's room.

4.065   Legler, Henry E.   "Library Work with Children." ALA
         Bulletin 4 (1911):240-246.

         Reviewing the concepts of society regarding children
         and the state of childhood, this writer postulated
         that children's services in the public library was a
         positive social force. Through the cooperative mode
         of children's work with schools and other agencies,
         which served children, the public library was
         evolving as a force for their educational and social
         growth.

4.066   Legler, Henry E.   "Library Work with Children: A
         Synoptical Criticism." ALA Bulletin 10 (1916) 205-
         208.

         Questioning whether children were overexposed to the
         reading of books, the writer presented constructive
         criticism of children's work. Should children read
         the latest books or just the classics was also
         asked.

4.067   Leigh, Robert D.   "P.L. I. and Library Work with
         Children." Top of the News. 6 (March, 1950):12-15.

         Discussed are the findings and recommendations of
         the Public Library Inquiry for work with children
         and youth. Although no formal study was made of
         children's work, Leigh declared it to be the
         classical success of the public library. From
         Berelson's report, 60% of library service is made to
         children and young people.

4.068   "Library and Schools." <u>Dial</u> 34 (1903):73-75.

Praising the work of public libraries in schools, it
was stated that the vision could be more expansive.
In an editorial, a case was presented for the
development of the school library as an entity in
the educational structure.

4.069   Lincoln, Helen L.   "The Head Librarian Looks at
Children's Work." <u>Wisconsin</u> <u>Library</u> <u>Bulletin</u> 43
(1947):90-91.

Opening with the fact that the children were the
adults of tomorrow, this statement served as
justification for children's work. The libraries of
the future would not lack financial or moral
support. To this were added the facts that the
library aided the development of adulthood and
citizenship.

4.070   Long, Harriet G. <u>Rich</u> <u>the</u> <u>Treasure</u>: <u>Public</u> <u>Library</u>
<u>Service</u> <u>to</u> <u>Children</u>. Chicago: American Library
Association, 1953.

Reflecting on the history of juvenile access to
libraries, the statement was made that children were
a part of the reading public in a community. The
public library sought to make books and reading a
part of the everyday life of the individual child.

4.071   McLenegan, Charles E.   "The Open Door, Through the
Book and the Library; Opportunity for Comparison and
Choice: Unhampered Freedom of Choice." <u>ALA</u>
<u>Bulletin</u> 6 (1912):127-132.

From the schools, the young acquired the skill to
read, but the library was the place of life-long
development. Learning to read was the means to
self-education. The true university of these days
was a collection of books.

4.072   Matthews, Caroline. "The Growing Tendency to Over-
emphasize the Children's Side." <u>Library</u> <u>Journal</u> 33
(1908):135-138.

Not all library advocates were supportive of the
emerging area of children's work. In this article,
the question was aired that pondered whether
children's work was the purview of the schools and
not the public library.

4.073   Miller, Herbert A. "The True Americanization of the
         Foreign Child." ALA Bulletin 13 (1919):130-132.

         The goal of Americanization of the foreign child was
         the development of a democratic character. To this
         end, the child should have respect for his parents,
         religion, mother country, and native language.

4.074   Moore, Annie Carroll. "The Bookshop for Boys and
         Girls." ALA Bulletin 11 (1917):168-169.

         Sharing her delight in her visit to the Bookshop for
         Boys and Girls, Moore gave her reactions to her
         first visit there. She visited the Bookshop on
         Christmas Eve with Miss Caroline Hewins.

4.075   Moore, Anne Carroll. "Library Membership as a Civic
         Force." ALA Bulletin 2 (1908):372-380.

         As a civic force in the community, library
         membership served as a positive operative in the
         development of citizenship in the young. Through
         library participation, children learned a respect
         for community property, a respect for others, and a
         sense of the common good.

4.076   Munn, Ralph. "The Social Significance of Library
         Work with Children." ALA Bulletin 24 (1930):348-
         351.

         Barriers existed to deflect from the significance of
         library work with children. First, there was the
         lack of good salaries and promotions for children's
         librarians. Second, there was a negative attitude
         towards the school library, which was a positive
         agent for reading and a cooperative operative with
         the public library. Third, there should be a bridge
         between children's and adult work.

4.077   Nesbitt, Elizabeth. A Child Went Forth. Pittsburgh:
         Carnegie Library School, 1941.

         Articulating what was recognized as the philosophy
         of children's services in the public library,
         Nesbitt made a case for the positive regard for the
         state of childhood. Whatever the physical
         circumstance of the child, the librarian should be
         aware of nurturing the hope of humanity through
         support of its intellectual and cultural
         development.

4.078   Nesbitt, Elizabeth. "Library Service to Children."
          Library Trends 3 (1954):118-128.

          Built on a positive foundation, children's work has
          acquired its proper place in public librarianship.
          From the founding objectives of the pioneers in
          children's work, current services are gleaning
          results. Therein is presented a current picture of
          children's work.

4.079   Olcott, Frances Jenkins. Library Work with
          Children. Chicago: American Library Association,
          1914.

          This was a manual of library economy. Covered in it
          were all of the essentials of children's work, such
          as, organization, interagency cooperation,
          programming, the children's librarian, and the
          children's room.

4.080   Power, Effie L. "The Children's Library in a
          Changing World." ALA Bulletin 22 (1928):375-381.

          After making their presence known in the public
          library, children were served with rooms, books, and
          trained librarians. For a changing world, all
          children in the country should have access to
          materials in the public library; book selection
          should be of a high quality; and there was a need
          for more trained professional staff.

4.081   Power, Effie L. "The Future of Library Work with
          Children: Part VI." Library Journal 62 (1937):19-
          20.

          Power's vision saw future success for children's
          librarianship, which came from the foundation of the
          past years. In the future, the chief administrator
          had to have a more active role in fostering the
          development of children's work.

4.082   Power, Effie L. Library Service for Children.
          Chicago: American Library Association, 1930.

          Developed as a resource in the ALA's Library
          Curriculum Study, this was the first official
          textbook designed in the instructional program for
          children's librarians. In the opening chapter.
          "Values in Library Work with Children," a
          comprehensive historical overview of the service was

presented. Covered in this resource were book
selection, juvenile collection development, the
children's room and or department, techniques of the
service, and its professional personnel.

4.083   Power, Effie L. "The Ounce of Prevention." Public
          Libraries 30 (1925):407-411.

          The task of children's work was to train the young
          to love books and the reading habit. If this task
          was accomplished, then there was "an ounce of
          prevention to offer against illiteracy . . ."

4.084   Power, Effie L. Work with Children in Public
          Libraries. Chicago: American Library Association,
          1943.

          This edition was an update and expansion of the
          1930, which was also produced by Power. Added to
          this volume was conceptionalization on children's
          work in the rural environment and on the importance
          of effective publicity for the specialty.

4.085   "Present Status of Library Work with Children." ALA
          Bulletin 16 (1922):21-22.

          Because of negative comments made at ALA
          Headquarter, a letter was sent to eighteen
          children's departments to glean views on the status
          of children's librarianship. It was felt that
          children's work was at a place to move forward and,
          truly, was a positive agent in librarianship.

4.086   Rathbun, Norma. "Children's Work and the
          Community." Wisconsin Library Bulletin 44
          (1948):155-156.

          To involve successfully, the community in the
          activities of children's work, the librarian should
          be the aggressor. In the community, the librarian
          should work with the Scouts, social welfare
          agencies, the schools, and businesses.

4.087   Robinson, Charles W. "From the Administrator's
          Desk." Top of the News 31 (1975):313-316.

Intellectual freedom is a concern of all librarians, especially in the school sector. To assure a proper perspective, the administrator should discuss the topic with children's librarians and be knowledgeable about children's materials.

4.088   Root, Mary E. S. "Children's Library Work." Library Journal 45 (1920):827-831.

One fundamental objective of children's work was to reach a good percentage of the young in the community with quality reading matter. The underlying goal was to create a core of readers for the adult department.

4.089   Sattley, Helen R. "Run Twice as Fast: Service to Children." American Libraries 2 (1971):843-849.

An educator discusses the recommendation that all services for children come under the purview of the school media centers.

4.090   Schimmel, Nancy. "Reading Guidance and Intellectual Freedom." Top and the News 31 (1975):317-320.

Reading guidance reflects how children's librarians talk to the young about books and how books are promoted in other ways. Reading guidance is the technique used to bring children and books together, without taking away their right to choose.

4.091   Scott, Carrie E. "The Future of Library Work with Children: A Symposium, Part II" Library Journal 61 (1936):819-820.

Whatever the future brought, the objectives of children's work would remain the same. Making good books available to all children, creating discriminating readers, and instilling an appreciation of the reading habit, as well as quality literature were the objectives of children's librarianship. New media would have an impact on children's services in the future, as well as, new techniques.

4.092   Scott, Edna Syman. "Inspirational Influence of Books in the Life of Children." ALA Bulletin 9 (1915):179-185.

If a book spoke to the heart or to the mind, firing
the enthusiasm, or stimulating thought, was it not
an inspirational influence? Inspirational books
represented a wide array of reading matter, because
it was an individual experience.

4.093   Sharp, E. Preston. "Youth! Libraries! Delinquency!"
        Top of the News 12 (October, 1955):11-16.

        As a society, we are beginning to think as a mass.
        There is a need for a call to intelligent
        individualism. In libraries, children can exercise
        their intelligent individualism through the reading
        material that they select.

4.094   Shea, Agatha L. "The Future of Library Work with
        Children: A Symposium, Part IX." Library Journal
        62 (1937):201-203.

        Over the years, the goals and objectives of
        children's service would not be changed, but the
        times would impact on the interest of the young. It
        would be a time when research would become a factor
        in children's librarianship.

4.095   Sherman, Clarence E. "The Future of Library Work
        with Children: A Symposium, Part III." Library
        Journal 61 (1936):919-922.

        For the public library, children's librarianship was
        an outstanding facet of its work. However, in the
        future, children's work would be impacted by radio,
        moving pictures, and the development of school
        libraries.

4.096   Smith, Bessie Sargeant. "Methods of Securing Better
        Reading." Public Libraries 10 (1905):171-173.

        The challenge to the public library was to encourage
        people to become better persons through better
        reading. To this end, the library should advertise
        through various media and by working with special
        interest groups in the community.

4.097   Smith, Irene. "Book Treasures and the Child."
        National Parent-Teacher 34 (November, 1939):33-35.

Even though many children were being served by
public libraries, great numbers were going unserved
in areas where service was limited. Quality
literature was published that children should
encounter while young; and this should be through
the public library.

4.098   Smith, Irene. "Wartime Outlook in Library Work with
Children." Library Journal 68 (1943):26-27.

Through books, children could find the glory of a
peaceful world for all people. As a result of the
war book funds were inadequate. There was a growing
shortage of children's librarians.

4.099   Smith, Lillian H. "The Future of Library Work with
Children: Part VII." Library Journal 62 (1937):20-
21.

Because the world was continually changing,
predicting the future of children's work was
difficult. However, if the children's librarians
continued to share the best in the realm of
literature, their place in librarianship would be
secured.

4.100   Smith, Nora Archibald. "Training the Imagination."
Outlook 64 (1900):459-461.

In education, there was the debate whether it should
cultivate faculties that are already operative or
not. The goal in education should be the full
development of individuality.

4.101   Stegman, Betty J., Editor. "Children's Services."
Illinois Libraries 52 (1970):323-393.

At this time, the crisis over whether children's
work belonged in the school or the public library
had the full attention of children's librarians. To
this end, a wide array of viewpoints were presented
on all facets of children's librarianship.

4.102   Tarbox, Ruth. "2001: A Library Odyssey." Top of
the News 25 (1969):144-146.

To the members of the Children's and Young Adults
Services Divisions, Tarbox was making a call for

change. The changes should include longer hours,
greater access to material, more emphasis on
multimedia, a restructuring of programming, and more
cooperation between the schools and public
libraries.

4.103   Tate, Binne L. "On Beyond 999Z: Patterns of
Library Service to Children of the Poor." In
Advance in Librarianship. V3. New York: Seminar
Press, 1972. pp. 1-14.

Under the rubric of outreach, library services are
being extended to the children of the poor. These
children are socially and environmentally
handicapped. Using services tailored to their
needs, the library is becoming an agent for positive
change.

4.104   Viguers, Ruth Hill. Margin for Surprise: About
Books, Children, and Librarians. Boston: Little,
Brown and Company, 1964.

These essays and speeches by Viguers deal with
criticism of children's books, the history of
children's books, children as readers and children's
librarianship. Running through the pieces are the
joy and power of books in the lives of children.

4.105   Waite, Helen Elmira. "Library Adventures for the
Youngest." Wilson Library Bulletin 20 (1945):328-
330.

Opening the children's room to pre-schoolers of the
age of four was a positive venture in establishing
the library habit. There was not a problem with
damage, disorder or loss. The young became
enthusiastic users of the library.

4.106   Washington, Bennetta B. "Before It Is Too Late."
Wilson Library Bulletin 43 (1968):140-145.

Are we losing the Black children, today? Every
institution which serves Black children should be
concerned with supplying positive images and role
models for them.

4.107   Wilson, Louis Round. "The Public Library as an
Educator." Library Journal 35 (1910):6-10.

By 1907, the public library had established itself
as an institutional factor in the dissemination of
popular education on the American scene. In its
educational mode, the public library should serve
first the child and then the adult in our society.
Serving in a cooperative manner with the schools the
public library was an operative in the education of
the child, while providing the adult population with
a source of continuing education for life.

4.108   Wyer, Malcolm G.   "Right Reading in Childhood."
         Iowa Library Quarterly 6 (1911):177-182.

         Gleaming an interest in reading quality literature
         was important to living a full and complete life.
         Classical literature had a civilizing influence and
         a social importance. Through the public library,
         were the positive effects of reading established,
         starting with the young child.

5

Client Group

5.001   Adams, Emma L.   "Methods of Children's Library Work
        as Determined by the Needs of the Children.--II."
        Library Journal 22 (1897):c28-31.

        Essential to children's work was an understanding of
        the needs of children which was gleaned from
        interaction with them, their instructors, their
        parents, and formal study.   Their most general need
        was for personal guidance.

5.002   Adams, John.   "Fathers and Children's Librarians."
        Illinois Libraries 6 (1924):60-66.

        Although children's librarians made great appeals to
        children and their mothers, fathers were neglected
        in the scheme of children's work.   Reading aloud was
        a special activity that parents should share with
        the children, especially fathers, as well.   For
        selection of juvenile books, whether for purchase or
        for borrowing, the fathers should refer to the
        children's librarian, who was the professional
        expert.

5.003   Benford, John Q.   "The Philadelphia Project."
        Library Journal 96 (1971):2041-2047.

        To ascertain the use of libraries by youth, the
        Philadelphia (Pa) project was developed.   It was the
        result of joint work of the Free Library, the public
        and parochial school systems, and several
        independent schools in Philadelphia.

5.004   Betzner, Jean.   "Patron Relations."   Wilson Library
        Bulletin 24 (1950):587-9; 593.

Children's use of the library was a voluntary
practice, where they exercised a choice. What the
library had to offer must nurture the individual.
Through readers' services the young had an adult
friend in the children's librarian who served as a
guide in the realm of children's literature.

5.005   Boothby, Ralph E. "Today's Children." New York
Libraries 13 (1932):129-132.

Impacting on the child of the day was change on
every front. "The child of today . . . [was]
responding merely to the special conditions of our
current changing civilization."

5.006   Burgess, Theodore. "Means of Leading Boys from the
Dime Novel to Better Literature." Library Journal
21 (1896):144-147.

Even the art of printing had contributed to evil in
the form of the dime novel. To determine the
influence of the dime novel, Burgess did a survey
among male students between the ages of light to
eighteen to discover the extent of dime novel
reading. With a thousand responses, he discovered
that half of the male students read the dime novel.

5.007   Burnite, Caroline. "The Youngest Children and Their
Books." Library Journal 28 (1903):215-217.

The object of this paper were the children in the
age range of four to nine years of age. The chief
suggestion was to separate the picture books from
the general juvenile collection.

5.008   Cloud, Eva. "Children's Work in the Small Library."
Public Libraries 25 (1920):65-67.

It is possible to cultivate a more personal and
intimate relationship with juvenile patrons in a
small public library. Because of the size of the
book collection, young children read more in the
classical vein of literature.

5.009   Coxe, Warren W. "Scientific Literature on the
Reading Interests of School Children." Library
Journal 57 (1932):9-15.

Teachers are trained to teach reading, while librarians in the educational process inculcate what to read or the reading of good literature. Through scientific studies, librarians learn about the reading interests of children, hence are better able to guide them. Focus should be on the studies that deal with the independent reading that children do.

5.010   Donahoe, Barbara. "Resident Library: A. I. Bowen Children's Center." Illinois Libraries 57 (1975):496-509.

For two years, the Shawnee Library (Carterville, IL) System operated the resident library at the A. I. Bowen Children's Center. Serving the mentally retarded was a challenging, exciting, and very demanding experience.

5.011   Dunn, Louise M. "The Reading of the Adolescent Girl." ALA Bulletin 11 (1917):162-167.

Reflective of the times, this presentation showed the adolescent girl as interested in homemaking, the romantic, and the dramatic. Expressed was the idea that reading became a channel for self-realization.

5.012   Elsmo, Nancy. "Make Room for Babies!" Wisconsin Library Bulletin 72 (1976):120-121.

What can you do to make the library more positive for babies and infants? High chairs, bouncing chairs, stroller, playpen and a baby box of books are all ways of making toddlers welcomed in the library.

5.013   "The Exceptional Child: A Symposium." Illinois Libraries 41 (1959):3-25.

The symposium papers were presented at the Illinois Library Association's annual conference in Chicago on November 8, 1957. The articles were "The Public Library Serves the Gifted Children," "The Library and the Exceptional Child," "Mentally Handicapped Children," and "Television and the Exceptional Child."

5.014   Fairchild, Edwin Milton. "Methods of Children's
         Library Work as Determined by the Needs of the
         Children - I." Library Journal 22 (1897):c19-27.

         The librarian should ask: "What do the children
         need; what are the best methods of doing for the
         children what they need; and how shall I succeed in
         getting my library to do this needed work?" For the
         young the library should provide an enrichment of
         life, enlargement of knowledge, and the
         establishment of the reading habit.

5.015   Fasick, Adele M. "Helping Children to Help
         Themselves Learn. Relevant Research." Top of the
         News 31 (1974):73-79.

         Preschool story hours should be an important facet
         in the shaping of the intellectual and creative
         growth of the young child. To this end, the
         professional should be aware of the relevant
         research about early childhood.

5.016   Field, Walter Taylor. "The Public Library and
         Children." Dial 42 (1907):67-69.

         There was a time when children were not welcomed in
         the public library. As the barriers to this age
         group dissolved, services have been tailored to
         encourage the young as a readership. Discussed were
         the importance of the story hour, the travelling
         library, the home library, and the various school
         plans in the public library.

5.017   Gymer, Rose C. "Personal Work With Children."
         Public Libraries 11 (1906):191-193.

         At the heart of children's work in public libraries
         was the reader's services aspect. To accomplish
         this objective, the children's librarian was
         required to know, as much as possible, about each
         child - the child's needs, abilities, and interest.
         Discussed, too, was the impact of reading clubs and
         storytelling on the young charge.

5.018   Harris, Rachel D. "Work with Children at the
         Colored Branch of the Louisville Free Public
         Library." Library Journal 35 (1910):160-161.

In 1905, the LFPL opened a branch, especially
designed to serve the black community of the city,
which was done with some reservation. At the
writing of this article, the branch was a positive
force in the community, but was in need of more
resources with which to serve its public.

5.019   Hatch, Alice K.   "The Every - Day Child and His
          Library." Scribner's Magazine 75 (1924):213-217.

          The hope of the country rested with the "Every -Day
          Child", who was of the middle class. Library work,
          whether a club, a story hour, or book selection, was
          stimulating and interesting.

5.020   Hobbs, Nicholas. "Recognizing the Gifted Child."
          Top of the News 28 (1971):41-42.

          Recognizing the gifted child was a challenge for
          librarians. Gifted children could be of any race or
          from any social strata. The gifted are as diverse,
          as humankind.

5.021   Jackson, Annie I. M.   "Present Day Objectives in
          Library Work with Children: Influences on Adult
          Reading." Library Journal 61 (1931):820-822.

          What the children's room of today did, impacted on
          the adults of the future. All children should be
          encouraged to read and to heighten their social
          awareness through books.

5.022   Johnson, Ferne, Editor. Start Early for an Early
          Start: You and the Young Child. Chicago: American
          Library Association, 1976.

          Starting with an overview of the young child, this
          work presents the methods, techniques and resources
          for working with this age group. The work is
          designed for parents, child care - providers,
          teachers and librarians.

5.023   Lanigan, Edith. "The Child in the Library."
          Atlantic 87 (1901):122-125.

          Through books and reading, a lonely child's world
          expanded. Reading the classics in his home library,
          an only child made friends with the characters and

shared in the adventures in the books, which he
read.

5.024   Lewerenz, Alfred S. "Children and the Public
          Library." Library Quarterly 1 (1931):152-174.

          To ascertain the type of child who used the branches
          of the Los Angeles (CA) Public Library, a special
          study was conducted. What the study found was that
          the child who used the public library was of a
          superior type, mentally and scholastically.

5.025   Long, Harriet. "Wider Horizons in Library Service
          to Boys and Girls." Top of the News 19 (December,
          1962):45-48.

          This period in history will be known as the "century
          of the child." On every front the child is the
          object of study in biology, anthropology, sociology,
          and psychology, which impacts on children's
          librarianship.

5.026   Martin, Clyde. "But How Do Books Help Children?"
          Library Journal 80 (1955):2333-2337.

          Everyone agreed that books are good for children,
          but does anyone know why or how do books help them?
          The ways in which the reading of fine books assist
          boys and girls in the task of growing into effective
          adults should be a part of the understanding of
          parents, librarians, and teachers.

5.027   Nesbitt, Elizabeth. "Books for Today's Children."
          Horn Book 24 (1948):95-99.

          One could not forget that a book was useless, unless
          a reader was attracted to it. For the different
          periods of childhood, children have varying reading
          needs.

5.028   Pinney, Marie. "The Exceptional Child and the
          Library." Library Journal 53 (1928):817-819.

          Whether the exceptional child was the prepsychotic
          child or the potential genius, the library had the
          responsibility of providing service to both. Every
          child should be viewed as an individual. This was a
          case in point for bibliotherapy.

5.029   Smith, Irene. "Human Side of Library Work with
         Foreign - Born Children." Library Journal 58
         (1933):865-868.

         The public library was an operative in the
         Americanization of the foreign - born children. Not
         only was it an educational agency, the public
         library served as a social and cultural institution.
         To serve this community of readers, books were used;
         stories told; and Reading clubs were held.

5.030   Spear, Grace B. "Children Are to Love." Wilson
         Library Bulletin 32 (1957):135-136.

         In the children's room of the public library,
         children are to love; books are to read; the
         children's librarian brings them together. But a
         children's room is even more. It is a meeting
         place, a workshop, a museum; and most of all it is a
         place where the child is the most important person.

5.031   Spear, Grace B. "Discipline Can Be Fun." Wilson
         Library Bulletin 31 (1956):168-169.

         Using book marks with doggerel, the children who
         need discipline are being challenged to conduct
         themselves better. The bookmarks started with Missy
         Bessie, Tardy Marty, Lazy Daisy, and Silly Willy.
         Others were added.

5.032   "A Story Of A Gang." Library Journal 40 (1915):486-
         487.

         In a neighborhood which was haunted by the antics of
         a gang, who also used the library as apart of its
         territory, the tale conveyed, how they were won as
         good patrons. Not giving in to fear, a children's
         librarian resorted to winning the gang's interest
         with hero tales and stories of adventure. When
         things in the neighborhood became worse, library use
         was restricted to card holders, which became the
         final facet in the surrender of the troop's terror.

5.033   "What Do Public Libraries Contribute to the
         Development of Children by the Work of the
         Children's Department?" Public Libraries 29
         (1924):365-371.

         A number of librarians responded to the question.
         Cited was the chief aim of children's work to make

available the best books to children. Then many
examples were given of the impact of children's work
on the young.

5.034   "What Type of Child Uses the Public Library?"
         Library Journal 62 (1937):730-734.

         Replicated was a study done in Los Angeles, CA, in
         1931. In three branches of the Denver (CO) Public
         Library a sample of 503 juvenile patrons were
         obtained. What was discovered was that most of the
         juvenile patrons were average students or above
         average.

5.035   White, Elizabeth. "Reaching the Parents Thru the
         Children - An Experiment in Publicity." Library
         Journal 42 (1917):522-523.

         For the Passaic (NJ) Public Library, juvenile users
         became an operative conduit to adult patrons. Each
         school age child was asked how the library served
         their family, as well as pertinent information of a
         demographic nature in the mass mailing of a letter.
         Through their responses, the students helped the
         library to promote its services, plus to glean
         information about its service area.

6

Collection Development

6.001   Ayres, Ernest F. "Not to be Circulated?" _Wilson Library Bulletin_ 3 (1929):528-529.

Taking exception with a list of books which were deselected by a librarian from a juvenile collection, the writer accused the profession of censorship. If a book served as a catalysis for the reading habit in children, it should be provided by the public library.

6.002   _Books for Boys and Girls: A Selected List_. Compiled by a Caroline M. Hewins. Boston: Press of Sockwell and Churchill, 1897.

The objective of this edition was to serve as a buying guide for small public libraries and parents. It included books to broaden the horizons of the young, to cultivate their imagination, and to add to their general knowledge. Textbooks were excluded.

6.003   _Books for the Young, A Guide for Parents and Children_. 2nd Edition. Compiled by C. M. Hewins. New York: Office of Publishers' Weekly, 1884.

Out of years of sharing books with the young, Hewins compiled a list of the classics of juvenile reading. The goal of the list was to elevate the quality of reading that young children did.

6.004   Bostwick, Arthur. "What Adults and Children Read." _Library Journal_ 21 (1896):444-446.

Using a system to isolate adult and juvenile circulation, the New York (NY) Free Circulating

Library was able to study the reading taste of these
two groups. Juveniles read more history, biography
and travel then the adults.

6.005   Burnite, Caroline. "The Standard of Selection of
         Children's Books." Library Journal 36 (1911):161-
         166.

         The aim of work with children was to inculcate and
         foster the practice of reading good books as a way
         of life. Secondary, to this was the function of
         children's work as a supplemental support to
         education. To the selection process, the
         professional must bring a knowledge of children,
         books, and values.

6.006   Bush, Mildred. "Methods of Book Selection."
         Illinois Libraries 13 (1931):150-152.

         Listed were the basic collection development tools
         for juvenile book selection. Criteria, that should
         be considered, were edition, physical format, and
         content. Important in the book selection process
         was a knowledge of children and of their reading
         habits.

6.007   Charters, W. W. "Changing Fashions in Dime Novel
         Substitutes." Library Journal 43 (1918):215-217.

         Replicating an earlier study which was done in 1907,
         a decade showed some differences in juvenile males
         choices for fiction. The dime novel of earlier
         years was the bane of the profession; and it was the
         objective to have youth read a better quality of
         literature.

6.008   Collar, Mildred A. "The Classification and
         Cataloging of Children's Books." Library Journal 28
         (1903):57-61.

         Working out a set of principles which would serve as
         a basis for a scheme of classification and
         cataloging for children's book was the object of
         this presentation. Central to this process would be
         a staff person who has experience with children's
         work and cataloging.

6.009   Curry, Charles M. "Standards in Children's
         Literature." Public Libraries 27 (1922):71-76.

To be of value, good books should have literary merit. Analyzed were fantasy, fairy tales, and biography. In the presentation, the writer stated that the main objective of library service was helping a patron to connect with the right book.

6.010   Cushman, Alice B. "Better Book Reviews Wanted."
         Wilson Library Bulletin 22 (1948):457, 463.

         Questioned was the variance that was found in the book reviews and annotations for juvenile books. There seemed to be a lack of critical reviewing of children's book.

6.011   Ely, Mary. "Our Present Problem." ALA Bulletin 8
         (1914):219-223.

         Throughout its history, children's work has served as a champion of quality reading materials for the young. Mediocrity in literature has always been a problem and was the focus of this discussion. To this was added the concerns of the appeal of the literature and its wide dissemination.

6.012   Endicott, Grace. "What Makes a Juvenile Book
         Harmful or Mediocre." New York Libraries 7
         (1920):97-101.

         Books could be negative operatives in the lives of young boys. Harmful books elevated crime and criminal activity to appear positive. Mediocrity was also harmful to young readers.

6.013   Flanagan, Leo. "Major Surgery with Toys!" Catholic
         Library World 46 (1975):422-425.

         At the Valley Falls Branch Library in Cumberland, Rhode Island, toys and various "nonbook" materials are important elements of the library's collection. Since these "nonbook" materials have been added, the circulation of books has increased.

6.014   Forbes, Mary A. "Children's Books: What
         Constitutes a Good Edition." Public Libraries 17
         (1912):118-120.

         When considering an edition, it was important to assess the purpose that the book was chosen to

fulfill, as well as the amount of money available.
During the selection process, the librarian should
be guided by the subject matter, physical makeup of
the book, and the illustrations.

6.015   Hazeltine, Alice I. "The Children's Librarian as a
Book Buyer." Library Journal 48 (1923):505-509.

For the children's librarian, one of the highlights
of the job was book selection. This should be
accomplished with certain facts and principles in
mind and to build the best collection within her
judgment.

6.016   Hektoen, Faith H. "In Our World of Books: What
Books for Sustenance?" Top of the News 22
(1965):109-114.

To be a good critic of what is quality reading for
children, a children's librarian should be committed
to reading as a life time pursuit. Effective
juvenile criticism of books comes from reading on
the adult spectrum; and the children's librarian
must read widely.

6.017   Hekton, Faith H. and Jeanne R. Rinehart, Editors.
Toys to Go: A Guide to the Use of Realia in Public
Libraries. Chicago: American Library Association,
1976.

Realia are toys, articles, and other three
dimensional objects that children handle,
manipulate, or play with to gain direct experience
and information about their environment. Learning
for young children occurs through play; and realia
are keys to this.

6.018   Herr, Marian. "Are Picture Books and Readers an
Asset or a Liability? Library Journal 72
(1947):1527-1528.

To ascertain, how other libraries addressed the need
for picture books and readers, a survey was made of
seven large and medium-sized cities: Akron,
Cleveland, Los Angeles, Newark, Rochester, St. Paul,
and Toledo. For most of the libraries, these
categories of books consumed up to 30% of their
budgets. The responses did not address, whether
this was an asset or liability.

6.019   Hewins, Caroline M. "Children's Books." Public
          Libraries 1 (1896):190-191.

          This lecture was presented to the students of the
          Pratt Institute (Brooklyn, NY) Library School. It
          signalled a call for reading as a means of elevation
          for young readers.

6.020   Hewins, Caroline M. "What You Can Get Out of a
          Henty Book." Wisconsin Library Bulletin 2
          (1906):69-70.

          Critics and librarians differed on the use of Henty
          books with children. Hewins read them for herself
          and believed that they were a good starting place in
          some studies.

6.021   Hunt, Clara W. "The Classification of Children's
          Story Books." Library Journal 27 (1902):65-68.

          At the Newark (NJ) Free Public Library, the decision
          was made to classify storybooks by subject.
          Presented in detail was the steps in this process.

6.022   "Interesting Evidence upon Books Popular with Young
          People." Wisconsin Library Bulletin 7 (1911):188-
          89.

          Over the years, educators and librarians have been
          interested in what young people voted as popular
          titles that they enjoyed. Herein, were samples of
          students' choices of their favorite books.

6.023   Jordan, Alice M. "Children's Classics." Horn Book
          23 (1947):9-17.

          Presented was a list of books to which children
          should be exposed in childhood. Each title had been
          read by a generation of the young and was adopted by
          another.

6.024   Kruse, Ginny Moore. "Select Carefully for Children:
          Hands-on, Printed and Consulting Helps are
          Available." Wisconsin Library Bulletin 70
          (1974):293-294.

          The hands-on method is the best way of selecting new
          juvenile titles. When hands-on is not possible,

there are some excellent print sources of reviews to aid the children's librarian. Lastly, there are the services of consultants.

6.025   Latimer, Louise P. "They Who Get Slapped." *Illinois Libraries* 6 (1924):49-54.

Reviewing the negative allegations which confronted children's librarians on the professional scene, the writer stated that these defective ideas should not deflect from the professional campaign for quality in literature. Children's librarians should be ever mindful of mediocrity, popular writers, untalented creators of children's books, and the formula books, all of which were a part of the plague on the literary scene.

6.026   Mason, Anna P. "Children's Books for Truth and Beauty." *Library Journal* 49 (1924):313-316.

At the fore in children's librarianship was the crusade for quality materials in the realm of children's literature. Making a case that the early cultivation of preference for the best books should be an objective of children's work with young children, the writer supported this view as being as important as learning reading skills. Then a survey was presented of what represented quality in the realm of children's literature.

6.027   Moore, Anne Carroll. "Children's Books and Their Proper Selection." *Publishers' Weekly* 105 (1924):1690-1694.

In a presentation before booksellers, Anne Carroll Moore suggested that the label "juvenile" should be taboo. Questioned also were the number of series books.

6.028   Moore, Anne Carroll. *My Roads to Childhood: Views and Reviews of Children's Books.* New York: Doubleday, Doran and Company, Inc., 1939.

Composed of three works, which were originally published separately and other material, *My Roads to Childhood* reflected Anne Carroll Moore's reminiscences, opinions on the whole spectrum of juvenile publications, and children's reading. Using the concept of roads through her personal and professional life, Moore wove her ideas and

perspectives into a thoughtful and stimulating work
for the realm of children's librarianship.

6.029   Morrisey, Elizabeth L. "The Essentials of a Good
        Book for Children." Public Libraries 11 (1906):548-
        549.

        Found in the best books for children should be
        ideals, as well as ideas. Good books should have a
        wholesome viewpoint, excite wonder, and stimulate
        thought, and have a moral.

6.030   Mumford, Edward W. "Choosing Books for Boys and
        Girls." Illinois Libraries 3 (1921):48-50.

        Taken from a presentation before the ABA was this
        criteria for analyzing series books. Questioned
        were the heroes, the activities, the language, and
        the portrayal of adults in series stories. All
        adults who brought books for the young were
        encouraged to read them before sharing the books
        with children.

6.031   Pearson, E. L. "The Children's Librarian Versus
        Huckleberry Finn: A Brief for the Defense."
        Library Journal 32 (1907):312-314.

        This was a case being made for having Tom Sawyer and
        Huckleberry Finn as a part of juvenile book
        collections. Children's librarians had been
        debating their inspirational value.

6.032   Richards, Laura. What Shall the Children Read?
        Illustrated by C. B. Falls. New York: D. Appleton
        - Century Company, 1939.

        Lamenting the structuring of the reading readiness
        syndrome in the young, the writer desired a return
        to the development of the child's abilities during
        the pre-school period. Stated was the fact that
        children as young as four should be taught the
        alphabet, for the alphabet held the key to the whole
        reading spectrum.

6.033   Silva, Mary E. "Book Reviewing for Book Selection."
        Wilson Library Bulletin 25 (1951):368-371.

Book reviewing equalled book selection. To the act
of book reviewing, the children's librarian should
bring a strong background steeped in general
knowledge and with professional reading. There
could not be any book reviewing without a wide
background of reading.

6.034   Skiff, Margaret S. "We Work as a Team in Selecting
         Books." Library Journal 80 (1955):948-956.

         At the Cuyahoga County (OH) Public Library, public
         and school libraries work as a team on collection
         development. Explained is its book selection
         process.

6.035   Smith, Jean Gardiner. "Big Town and Little, What
         Books Shall You Buy?" Top of the News 12 (March,
         1956):15-18.

         Book selection is apart of the work for all
         librarians. Good book reviews convey what the book
         is about and how it will fit in a collection. It is
         up to the wisdom of the librarian to select it or
         not.

6.036   Spain, Frances Lander. "The Selection and
         Acquisition of Books for Children." Library Trends
         3 (1955):455-461.

         This was a discussion of the methods of acquisition
         of books for children by public libraries and by
         public school libraries. Whether accomplished by
         committee, monthly meetings or selection tools, the
         reviewing of books is done in a thorough manner.

6.037   Straus, Esther. "Some Recent Tendencies in
         Children's Literature." Public Libraries 17
         (1912):252-256.

         The majority of literature for the juvenile was
         marked by the commonplace. During the selection
         process, the librarian should be mindful whether the
         book would serve as a tool in the child's
         development.

6.038   Van Buren, Maud. "Children's Magazines." Wisconsin
         Library Bulletin 8 (1912):35-36.

From the adults who worked with the young and
parents, was coming the request for more juvenile
periodicals. The writer reviewed the market and
felt that the three best were St. Nicholas, Youth's
Companion, and Popular Mechanics.

7

Readers' Services

7.001   Baker, Augusta. "Pioneer in the War on Poverty:
        NYPL." Library Journal 89 (1964):3376-3379.

        By the very nature of the racial make-up of its
        community, the New York (NY) Public Library has been
        a pioneer in the war on poverty. First, there were
        the European immigrants, then in the 1920's came the
        Blacks from the south.

7.002   Bell, Bernice W. "The Colored Branches of the
        Louisville (KY) Free Public Library." ALA Bulletin
        11 (1917):169-173.

        The public library started services through the
        Black branches in 1905. In the Eastern and Western
        branches most of the services were designed for the
        youth in the communities.

7.003   Benjamin, Selma. "How Many Blocks to New York?"
        Library Journal 93 (1968):265-266.

        To introduce "nonbookish" children to reading, a
        hobby club was formed for eight to twelve year olds
        in the Venice branch of the Los Angeles (CA) Federal
        Project.

7.004   Blaha, Linda. "There's a Pet in My Book Bag!" Top
        of the News 31 (1974):90-94.

        Teaming up with the Animal Protective League, the
        Parma Regional Branch of the Cuyahoga County (OH)
        Public Library held a contest for pets. Not only
        did it furnish homes for animals, but gave the
        library excellent exposure in the community.

7.005   Bruner, Bernice. "Creative Activities in a Public
         Library Children's Room." Illinois Libraries 40
         (1958):649-654.

         The library can be a place where children follow
         their creative pursuits. The activities include
         puppets, writing, storytelling, dramatic play and
         crafts.

7.006   Bubb, Ethel. "Reading Without a Purpose."
         Libraries 31 (1927):338-341.

         To read for the fun and joy of the experience is
         reading without a purpose. It is the responsibility
         of the children's librarian to introduce to the
         young the pleasures of books.

7.007   Burnite, Caroline. "Sequences in Children's
         Reading." Public Libraries 20 (1915):160-165.

         It was easier to guide and direct the sequence of
         reading for the young child, then the older one.
         Starting with fairy tales, the younger reader moved
         on to fiction. After the age of twelve, there was
         more variety in the choices of reading matter by the
         older reader.

7.008   Burr, Elizabeth. "Children's Library Service in
         Wisconsin's Public Libraries . . . " Wisconsin
         Library Bulletin 56 (March-April, 1960):83-86.

         This is an overview of children's work in the state
         for the year. Operating under the goal of imbuing
         children with a love of reading, the public
         libraries in Wisconsin were expanding children's
         services.

7.009   Casey, Phyllis A. "Playing Games in the Children's
         Room." Library Journal 56 (1931):1058-1059.

         Using games to stimulate an interest in reading and
         to teach reading skills, was the object of this
         project. The games that were used were puzzles,
         secret codes, and authors.

7.010   Children's Library Yearbook: Number Four. Compiled
         by The Committee on Library Work with Children of

The American Library Association. Chicago:
American Library Association, 1932.

The fourth volume of this publication was divided
into three sections: 1) developing children's
reading interests, 2) the children's librarian and
3) library service to special groups. Under special
groups there was a commentary by Langston Hughes.

7.011   Clarke, Elizabeth Porter. "Story-Telling, Reading
           Aloud and Other Special Features of Work in
           Children's Rooms." Library Journal 27 (1902):189-
           190.

           A survey was done to ascertain the programming used
           to introduce literature to children. First and
           foremost was the story hour. Reading aloud was also
           popular. Lectures, clubs, and games were also being
           utilized.

7.012   Clements, Zacharie and Leon Burrell. "An Interview
           with Two Hip Reading Educators on How Librarians
           Others Can Put the Zing Back into Sleep-Time Summer
           and Year-Round Reading Programs." Wilson Library
           Bulletin 47(1973):687-690.

           Two educators tell librarians to make the library a
           source of entertainment and recreation first, then
           youth will absorb the positive from the reading
           experience.

7.013   Compton, Charles H. "Typical Day in a Children's
           Room." Wisconsin Library Bulletin 40 (1944):116-
           118.

           Presented were the statistics for a typical day in
           the St. Louis Public Library's children's room. On
           November 1, 1943, 4,487 books were circulated to
           2,407 children. A detailed analysis was made of the
           total array of books that were circulated on that
           day.

7.014   Crane, Stanley D. "Putting on a Storybook Pet
           Show." Wilson Library Bulletin 30 (1955):624-625.

           The Brooklyn (NY) Public Library and a local
           department store cosponsored "A Storybook Pet Show."
           What led to this event was the desire of both
           agencies to keep children motivated to read books.
           The article gives the details of the projects.

7.015   Davidson, Letha M.   "Methods of Encouraging Young
         People to Read Good Literature." Wisconsin Library
         Bulletin 25 (1929):283-292.

         Children of today are treated as individuals; and it
         is the personal contact between the librarian and
         the child that is important. Other methods for
         bringing literature to the young are clubs, story
         hours, reading courses, puppet shows, book lists,
         visual aids, and working with schools.

7.016   Drennan, Henry. "Little Miracle on Chapel Street."
         American Education 2 (July, 1966):1-5.

         This is the story of 1580 Chapel Street, which is an
         offbeat library in New Haven, Connecticut.
         Innovative programming to meet community needs is at
         the heart of this library's services.

7.017   Durlin, Maud. "Picture Bulletins." Wisconsin
         Library Bulletin 3 (1907):57-59.

         Presented was a detailed guide for the creation of
         bulletin boards in the library. The purpose of a
         picture bulletin was to serve as a conduit to good
         reading.

7.018   Eastman, Linda A. "Methods of Work for Children:
         The Cleveland Library League." Library Journal 22
         (1897):686-688.

         To train the juvenile users to respect and to care
         for books, the Cleveland (OH) Public Library started
         the Library League. Captured in this article was
         the first meeting of the group, where five thousand
         youth attended.

7.019   Ellis, Elizabeth. "Instruction of School Children in
         the Use of Library Catalogs and Reference Books."
         Public Libraries 4 (1899):311-314.

         Having lessons on the use of the library for school
         children was the object of this presentation.
         Library instruction was suggested for students in
         the third grade. Then the article gave a detailed
         discussion of what should be taught, stressing the
         catalog, indices, and special reference tools.

7.020   Fenner, Phyllis R. "How's Your Memory, Pal? _Wilson_
        Library _Bulletin_ 17 (1943):801-803.

        Were children's specialists only sharing current
        books with young readers? There were many titles
        from the past that the young should experience.

7.021   Fowler, Bonnie Louise Shaw. "Children's Outreach
        Programs: Their Theories and Practices." MA
        Thesis, University of Chicago, 1976.

        This was a story of public library programs, which
        reach out into the community to serve children who
        would not otherwise be library users. The last
        section of this study is a survey of a number of
        children's outreach programs in the southeastern
        United States.

7.022   Frankenfield, Pearl. "Egg Trees Everywhere."
        Library _Journal_ 78 (1953):480-483.

        With the publication of the 1950 winner of the
        Caldecott Award, _The_ _Egg_ _Tree_, eggtrees have
        surfaced in many places. On the national scene,
        children's librarians have become the corps behind
        the egg tree celebration.

7.023   Fritz, Jean. "Parents: A Challenge to Librarians."
        Library _Journal_ 82 (1957):1077-1081.

        There are many ways in which librarians can reach
        out to parents. Working through the PTA, having
        workshops, using bulletin boards and doing special
        projects are all ways of reaching parents.

7.024   Geller, Evelyn. "Baltimore's Fine Fettle." _School_
        Library _Journal_ 18 (1972):32-36.

        Fines on juvenile books can be a deterrent to public
        library use. To this end and in harmony with the
        third Deiches report the Enoch Pratt (Baltimore, MD)
        Free Library, eliminated juvenile fines in an
        experimental project.

7.025   Geller, Evelyn. "This is my Beat." _School_ _Library_
        Journal 14 (1968):39-44.

Spending a day with Don Roberts of the Venice (CA)
Public Library was an encounter with a vital change
agent in motion. The staff of the Venice branch had
tapped every agency within its community for its
outreach services.

7.026   Greene, Jane. "Library Service to Migrants: Door
         County Library Migrant Program." Wisconsin Library
         Bulletin 62 (1966):19-22.

         During the summer of 1965, the Door County (WI)
         Library conducted a program for the migrant
         children. Through a Community Action Program grant,
         staff was hired; and materials were purchased for
         the project.

7.027   Gross, Elizabeth H. "Summer Reading Its Own
         Reward." Library Journal 80 (1955):1232-1234.

         Taking a side in the heated debate about summer
         reading programs, Elizabeth Gross of EPFL of
         Baltimore, Maryland was for them. To this end, she
         discussed some of the past reading programs, which
         were system-wide or tailored to a special community.

7.028   Hadlow, Ruth M. "The Children's Festival of the
         Chrysanthemun." Top of the News 14 (October,
         1957):29-30+.

         The Children's Department of the Cleveland (OH)
         Public Library planned a series of programs to
         celebrate world cultures. In 1956 the library
         celebrated "The Children's Festival of the
         Chrysanthemun" through art, dance, folklore and
         exhibits.

7.029   Harre, David. "The Alley Library." Top of the News
         24 (1968):208-211.

         Out of the request of five elementary school boys
         for a place to study grew the Alley Library in
         Washington, D.C. There was a Freedom School on
         Saturday afternoons, then tutoring sessions were
         added. To make the books that were collected more
         useful to the children, they were cataloged. It was
         an environment where chaos was encouraged to meet
         the temperament of the young users.

7.030   Harrison, Lucretia M.   "A Foreign Language Center
           for Children."   Top of the News 28 (1972):138-144.

           At the Hempstead (NY) Public Library, there was
           opened a Foreign Language Center for children, who
           were bilingual or studying English as a second
           language. This report was a record of the operation
           and guidelines for starting such a project.

7.031   Hatch, Bertha.   "Reference Work with School
           Children."   Wisconsin Library Bulletin 15
           (1919):173-176.

           To cope with the communication problems that
           juveniles pose in reference service, this article
           made a series of practical suggestions. Foremost in
           effecting positive reference work with children was
           the development of some mode of communication with
           the teacher. Knowledge of the juvenile collection
           and instruction of individuals or classes are key
           facets in reference services for the young.

7.032   Haviland, Virginia.   "The Quiz Invades the Library."
           Wilson Library Bulletin 21 (1946):160-161, 172.

           At the Phillips Brooks Branch of the Boston (MA)
           Public Library, a quiz game was started in the
           summer of 1945. Initially, it dealt with books,
           then expanded to include geography, history, and
           spelling.

7.033   Hawk, Fran.   "Recommended by the Junior Critics."
           Top of the News 32 (1975):73-76.

           To maintain the interest of junior high school
           students in reading, the Wellesley (MA) Free Library
           started a circle for junior critics. The object of
           the project was to have the junior critics review
           the library's books for their peers.

7.034   Hawthorne, Hildegarde.   "How to Form a Reading
           Club."   St Nicholas 41 (June, 1914):734-736.

           Detailed instructions were presented for forming a
           Reading Club. Besides reading quality literature,
           members should be encouraged to read-aloud, to
           discuss the books, and to write book reports. On
           the reading agenda should be fiction and nonfiction
           works on each topic or of each author.

7.035   Hazeltine, Mary Emogene. "How to Conduct a Dramatic
           Reading." Wisconsin Library Bulletin 11 (1915):11-
           17.

           Through dramatic reading, books were given life;
           quality literature stressed; and a pleasant time
           could be had by all who were involved. This paper
           was a manual of instruction for dramatic readings,
           along with suggestions of good plays for
           presentation.

7.036   Hewins, Caroline M. "Our Vacation Book Talks."
           Public Libraries 5 (1900):231-233.

           To help the youth through the summer months, Hewins
           conducted sessions with book talks. Although
           response was small, the venture was positive.
           Included was an account of the books used in each
           session.

7.037   Hewins, Caroline M. "Reading Clubs for Older Boys
           and Girls." Pedagogical Seminary 16 (1909):325-330.

           Starting with the year - 1881, Hewins related the
           details of various Reading Clubs for youth that had
           been held at the Harford (CT) Public Library. Used
           were the techniques of reports, reading-aloud and
           dramatic reading.

7.038   Hewins, Caroline M. "Report on Children's Reading."
           Library Journal 23 (1898):35-39.

           Reports came from 125 libraries in response to a
           survey of seventeen questions. Public libraries
           were asked if they provided children's reading
           rooms.

7.039   Hewins, Caroline M. "Report on Reading of the
           Young." Library Journal 18 (1893):251-253.

           Out of a 160 surveys, there were 146 replies to the
           series of questions asked. Inquiries included
           information on age limits and separate reading rooms
           for children.

7.040   Hewins, Caroline M. "Some Things Done in Hartford,
           Connecticut Public Library." Public Libraries 12
           (1907):86-89.

Penning a letter to the Chicago (IL) Public Library,
Hewins described the children's room, the activities
in children's services, and the composition of the
juvenile patrons. The object of the presentation
was to serve as a reference point for children's
work in the branches of a metropolitan library
system.

7.041   Hill, Marjorie B. "Lois Lenski Day at Warder."
        Library Journal 79 (1954):756-757.

        Sharing expenses with the local Association for
        Childhood Education, the Warder Public Library of
        Springfield, OH invited Lois Lenski to their city to
        celebrate the naming of the children's room in her
        honor. A series of events were planned to make the
        day a great occasion.

7.042   Hunt, Clara W. "Arousing an Interest in the Great
        Classics for Children." New York Libraries 3
        (1912):47-51.

        Reading the classics should be cultivated in the
        young. To this end, early in childhood every child
        should be introduced to great literature through the
        technique of reading - aloud.

7.043   Hunt, Clara W. "Children's Book Week: A
        Librarian's Point of View." Publisher's Weekly 100
        (1921):69-71.

        Addressing the book trade on the occasion of
        Children's Book Week, Hunt stated that it was a
        great opportunity for advertising for juveniles.
        Publicized should be quality books, whether current
        or classic.

7.044   Hunt, Clara W. "Some Means By Which Children May Be
        Led to Read Better Books." Library Journal 24
        (1899):147-149.

        The aim of the children's room is to induce the
        young to read quality literature. To this end,
        there should be used bulletin boards, reading list,
        selection of a positive book collection, displays,
        and sensitive children's librarians.

7.045   James, Jeanne S. "Starting a Library Stamp Club."
         Wilson Library Bulletin (1970):645-649.

         Stamp collecting can lead to many things, since
         there is a stamp for every subject under the sun.
         Library stamp clubs will attract the young.

7.046   Jenks, Carolyn K. "Get Out of the Rut -
         Experiment!" Library Journal 99 (1974):1458-1459.

         At the Durham (NH) Library, they did not do a summer
         reading club, but experimented with programming.
         For seven weeks, they programmed with stories,
         puppetry and crafts, which proved to be much to the
         liking of the young patrons.

7.047   Kessler, Helen T. "Summer Reading Clubs." Illinois
         Libraries 48 (1966):740-743.

         Discussed are the summer reading clubs of the Peoria
         (IL) Public Library. Although summer reading clubs
         maybe old hat for professionals, there are always a
         corps of children for whom they are new.

7.048   Kimmel, Margaret Mary." Library - Program =
         Storehouse?" Top of the News 32 (1975):51-58.

         Citing program objectives for an array of library
         projects, Kimmel gave the rationale for such
         endeavors. Programming allows a library to become
         more than a storehouse of books.

7.049   Klumb, David and others. "A Public Library Works
         with the Retarded." Wisconsin Library Bulletin 67
         (1971):34-36.

         In the Mead (Sheboygan, WI) Public Library, the
         librarians worked with two groups of the retarded.
         Using stories, films, filmstrips and realia, they
         helped to expand the horizons of these special
         library patrons.

7.050   Korkmas, Sister Ann. "Project 'Look at Me!'"
         Catholic Library World 45 (1973):158-160.

         "Project Look at Me!" was conducted by the Dallas
         (TX) Public Library's Community Education Office.
         Its goal is to foster literacy needs by teaching

communication skills of listening and speaking.
Using photography and tapes, the project worked with
the literacy problem of minority youth between the
ages of 10-13.

7.051   Ladenson, Alex. "Chicago: The Public LIbrary
          Reaches Out." Wilson Library Bulletin 43
          (1969):875-881.

          For two years, the Chicago (IL) Public Library had
          developed programs of outreach in underprivileged
          neighborhoods of the city. Through its outreach
          services, adults, youth, and children were served.

7.052   Larrick, Nancy. "Setting the Stage for Reading."
          Catholic Library World. 47 (1976):286-287.

          Creating a bright, cozy atmosphere in the library
          should be one of the objectives of the librarian.
          Integrating books, media and activities will have
          great appeal to young patrons.

7.053   Lehane, Veronica M. "These Young Readers Know What
          They Like." Library Journal 80 (1955):1240-1243.

          For the Spring Book Club, the librarian expanded the
          program, by requiring that the children submit
          written reports of their reading. To this was added
          a Spring Book Festival where the young patrons chose
          the books that they liked.

7.054   McClung, Quantrille. "A Poetry Circle as a
          Substitute for the Story Hour." Public Libraries 29
          (1924):453-456.

          In a community, where storytelling had become a fad,
          the librarian developed a poetry circle. Poetry was
          read; poets studied; original poetry written; and
          special readers were presented.

7.055   McCune, Brenda and Jane M. Singh. " . . . it
          happens the year 'round . . . ." Top of the News 28
          (1972):254-261.

          Through the joint efforts of the Schlow-Memorial
          Library of State College, PA and the university, a
          Book Magic Hour was presented. Using a variety of
          themes, university students presented special

programs weekly on Saturday morning for youngsters
four to twelve. There were dancing, creative arts,
storytelling, chalk talks, puppet shows, movies,
drama, and etc.

7.056   Mahar, Mary Helen. "Implications of the Library
          Services Act for Services to Children and Young
          People." ALA Bulletin 53 (1959):118-122.

          Through projects under the Library Services Act,
          work with children and young adults is being
          expanded, especially in rural America. The key to
          this has been bookmobile services.

7.057   Martignoni, Margaret E. "Bring Books and Children
          Together in the Library." Wilson Library Bulletin
          28 (1953):179-181.

          Although a child's reading choices are an individual
          matter, there are standard guides that suggest
          reading taste for a given age group. A librarian
          can couple a child with a book at any age, if the
          medium reflects the child's current interest.

7.058   Milliken, Marie Hammond. "Library Clubs for Boys
          and Girls." Library Journal 36 (1911):251-253.

          For the Cleveland (OH) Public Library, the library
          clubs served as a vehicle for strengthening its
          effectiveness as an educational and social outlet in
          the community. Each club was structured around a
          formal organizational pattern, which pursued the
          collective interests of the members through books
          and information. Although the library club program
          was under the supervision of a professional, the
          groups were facilitated by volunteers.

7.059   "Miss Hewins 'Goop' Verse." Wisconsin Library
          Bulletin 1 (1905):79.

          Since the care of books was important and stressed,
          Miss Hewins' "Goop" verse was widely disseminated.
          The GOOPS they wet their fingers/To turn the leaves
          of books,/And then they crease the corners down/And
          think that no one looks,/They print the marks of
          dirty hands,/Of lollipops and gum,/On picture-book
          and fairy-books,/As often as they come./ARE YOU A
          GOOP? ? ?

7.060   Moon, E. E. "High John." Library Journal 93
         (1968):147-155.

         High John is the library for Fairmount Heights,
         Maryland, as well as research laboratory for the
         School of Library and Information Services at the
         University of Maryland. It is a multi-purpose
         project to take library services to the unserved.

7.061   Moore, Annie Carroll. "The Place of Pictures in
         Library Work for Children." Library Journal 25
         (1900):159-162.

         Expressed was the opinion that a good picture
         collection was as necessary as a good book
         collection. Suggestions were made for permanent
         artwork in the children's room, as well as the type
         for bulletins and exhibits.

7.062   Moore, Annie Carroll. "Work with Children from
         Institutions for the Deaf and Dumb." Library
         Journal 35 (1910):158-159.

         Serving all facets of the community's juvenile
         population, the New York (NY) Public Library through
         its branches reached out to the hearing disabled.
         Library visits and story hours were conducted for
         these special young patrons.

7.063   Moore, Evva L. "Picture-Work in Children's
         Libraries - II." Library Journal 25 (1900):67-68.

         There were three objectives for using pictures in
         children's librarianship. The first was to increase
         the young's appreciation and enjoyment of great art.
         Secondly, picture bulletins could present new topics
         of interest. The third objective was to use
         pictures in school work.

7.064   Morgan, Madel, Suellen Morrison and Larry Diener.
         "Choctaw Performing Arts Tour." Top of the News 31
         (1975):178-181.

         As a part of the Summer Reading Program, there was a
         performing arts tour of Choctaw culture, featuring
         song and dance, in Mississippi. It was a positive
         approach of sharing Native America culture with the
         general public.

7.065   Newcomb, Nadine J. "The Good Start Program:
          Reading Readiness in Action." Library Journal 99
          (1974):541-545.

          At the Glassboro (NJ) Public Library, there evolved
          a special program for pre-schoolers and their
          mothers, which was devoted to reading readiness.
          Twice a week, the project presented a new skill for
          the pre-schoolers to learn, with which the mothers
          could work during the week.

7.066   Nicholas, Lillian and Pauline Ames. "Summer Reading
          Plans: A Debate." Library Journal 65 (1940):326-
          330.

          Questioned were the rationale and value of summer
          reading plans/games. For a core of children's
          librarians, they merited the time and benefit gained
          on all fronts from encouraging recreational reading.
          On the other hand, some children's librarians saw
          them in a negative light in terms of quality, time,
          circulation, and etc.

7.067   Nourse, Dorothy. "Circuses for Circulation."
          Library Journal 71 (1946):1793-1794.

          At the East Boston (MA) Branch, the staff created a
          circus motif for the Spring Book Festival. The
          final project in the celebration was a pet show
          which was opened to card holders of the branch.

7.068   Ogilvie, Phillip S. "Library Orientation" Library
          Journal 82 (1957):1081-1084.

          Introducing children to the public library was the
          object of this article. A detailed orientation
          session was presented, with a tour of the library
          and discussion of the card catalog the focus of the
          visit.

7.069   Plummer, Mary W. "The Christmas Book Exhibit in
          Libraries." Library Journal 36 (1911):4-9.

          For the public, the library provided guidance in the
          selection of gift-books, regarding content, edition,
          and illustration. Surveying the professional arena,
          it was found that a number of libraries performed
          this service and that other libraries were adding
          it. From the survey was gleaned the reasoning for
          such an effort and the results.

7.070   Polette, Nancy and Marjorie Hamlin. <u>Reading</u>
        <u>Guidance</u> <u>in</u> <u>a</u> <u>Media</u> <u>Age</u>. Metuchen, NJ: The
        Scarecrow Press, Inc., 1975.

        Presented are various approaches for sharing
        children's books with young readers. This is a
        guide for parents, teachers, librarians, and media
        specialists.

7.071   Potter, Inez. "Ways of Interesting Children in
        Reading." <u>Illinois</u> <u>Libraries</u> 7 (1925):112-115.

        Many were the ways of introducing and interesting
        the young in reading. Working through community
        groups and organization was important. Having in
        the library pleasant surroundings for the children
        and activities that challenged them were other
        devices to induce reading as a positive pursuit.

7.072   Potter, Marjorie F. "Is This a Library?" <u>Wilson</u>
        <u>Library</u> <u>Bulletin</u> 18 (1944):676-677.

        On Thursday afternoons for a couple of hours, the
        seven to ten year olds were allowed to have a
        "playhour" in the Albany (NY) Public Library. There
        the children played games, drew, and dressed-up in
        the company of volunteers and several librarians.

7.073   Power, Leah. "Publicity and the Children's
        Department." <u>Wilson</u> <u>Library</u> <u>Bulletin</u> 9 (1934):63-
        69.

        Serving as the best operative for publicity was a
        satisfied reader, who was hooked by the enthusiasm
        of the librarian. To this was added all of the
        techniques of readers' services, such as story
        hours, clubs, and class visits. Examples were
        shared of the publicity that was used in the Warsaw
        (IN) Public Library.

7.074   Quimby, Harriet and others. "Brooklyn Groves." <u>Top</u>
        <u>of</u> <u>the</u> <u>News</u> 26 (1970):283-287.

        Four staff members of the Brooklyn (NY) Public
        Library shared their innovative program techniques
        with their peers. Used to do traditional and non-
        traditional programming was a whole gamut of media.

7.075   Robbins, Margaret. "No Roses for Harry." Library
         Journal 91 (1966):1587-1590.

         In May, 1965, the North Manhattan Project was
         launched by the New York (NY) Public Library at the
         Countee Cullen branch in Harlem. The staff and the
         services were expanded through the funds of the
         project.

7.076   Root, Mary E. S. "Children and Library Tools."
         Library Journal 40 (1915):24-27.

         Through a practical demonstration, librarians were
         shown how to conduct Bibliographic Instruction for
         the primary grades. In the session the children
         were introduced to the card catalog and reference
         tools using a lecture and a practice sequence.

7.077   Root, Mary E. and Adelaide B. Maltby. "Picture
         Bulletins in the Children's Library." Library
         Journal 27 (1902):191-194.

         Through a survey, the use of picture bulletins and
         artwork was ascertained. Picture bulletins were
         used to supplement school work, advertise fiction
         and non-fiction, as well as to celebrate special
         occasions.

7.078   Rossell, Beatrice Sawyer. "When Children and Books
         Get Together." National Parent-Teacher 36 (October,
         1941):11-13.

         Anecdotes of effective readers' services were given,
         where young readers find the information that meets
         their reading needs. Presented were the responses
         to librarians as service personnel.

7.079   Schroether, Marian. "Promoting Reading for Fun."
         Illinois Libraries 48 (1966):705-707.

         Children's librarians have the nicest of jobs -
         convincing boys and girls that reading is fun.
         Although all children's librarians share this common
         objective, what reading guidance technique they use
         is an individual matter.

7.080   Shaw, Spencer. "Children's World/USA." Library
         Journal 90 (1965):1996-1997.

Children's World/USA was apart of the library
exhibit at the 1964-65, New York World's Fair.
Furnished with books and multi media, the library
provided parents and children an ideal place to
browse. Story hours and film programs were held on
a daily basis.

7.081   Siminow, Alyce. "Mead's Toybrary is Thriving."
Wisconsin Library Bulletin 70 (1974):168-169.

The Mead (Sheboygan, WI) Public Library opened a Toy
Lending Library. Served through the library are
children from pre-school to the sixth grade. Not
only are the toys for fun, but enhance the
intellectual growth and development of children, as
well.

7.082   Solis-Cohen, Leon M. "Library Work in the Brooklyn
Ghetto." Library Journal 33 (1908):485-488.

Responding to an influx of Russian Jews, the BPL
opened a branch in the Brownsville area. For the
librarians, the challenge was working with a
community which was new to the American scene and
ideas. It proved to be a public which was very
responsive to the services of the public library,
especially the children.

7.083   Stearns, Lutie E. "Report On Reading for the
Young." Library Journal 19 (1894):81-87.

Surveying almost two hundred public libraries, there
were a hundred and forty-five replies. Gleaned from
the survey was information on age limits, juvenile
use of the library, teachers' cards, classroom
collections, and separate facilities for the young.

7.084   Stotz, Doris. "Community Action - Action for
Children: An Interview with Thelma Bell." Top of
the News 24 (1968):190-197.

The Community Action Program was the Enoch Pratt
(Baltimore, MD) Free Library's participation in the
War on Poverty. In old houses in the inner city,
library rooms were opened where books were
circulated, where storyhours were held and where
children could play, as well as learn.

7.085   Tollefson, H. A. "A Library - Pivot for a
          Community." Childhood Education 36 (1960):410-414.

          For the Louisville (KY) Free Public Library, the
          goal of serving children was the creation of the
          adult patron of the future. Children who came to
          the library were made to feel welcome and wanted by
          this agency. Programs were planned for juveniles
          from pre-school to eight grade.

7.086   "TREES and FREDD"   American Libraries 6 (1975):19-
          21.

          In Bloomfield, CO, they have designed a toy library
          for the mentally handicapped child, which is called
          TREES (Teaching Resources for Educating Exceptional
          Students). Another program of the Connecticut State
          Library for the Disabled is a special bookmobile,
          which is called FREDD (Free Resources for Educating
          the Developmentally Disabled).

7.087   Tyler, Anna C. "Library Reading Clubs for Young
          People." Library Journal 37 (1912):547-550.

          For the older primary school students, reading clubs
          had more appeal, then the name story hour.
          Following the club format, they were either formally
          or informally organized, but always developed to
          reflect the interest of the members. Since the
          interests of girls and boys differ during this
          period, the reading clubs were formed according to
          sex. Utilized as one effective technique for
          conducting the sessions was reading - aloud.

7.088   Van Buren, Maud. "Junior Civic League." Wisconsin
          Library Bulletin 6 (1910):133-136.

          During school visits, the librarian invited the
          children to join the Junior Civic League which
          served as a vehicle for developing civic and home
          pride. Through the library, the children are
          registered; seeds distributed; and germane books
          were circulated.

7.089   Walter, Virginia and Nancy Schimmel. "Looking
          Beyond His Own Block." Wilson Library Bulletin 45
          (1970):163-167.

          Although it is the goal to share books of the Black
          experience with inner city children, their horizons

should be expanded to meet the whole world of
childhood as presented through books. Included are
some ways of expanding the children's views of the
world through books.

7.090   Webb, Marian A. "A Survey of Children's Reading."
        ALA Bulletin 26 (1932):728-733.

        From the Public Library of Fort Wayne, IN, came
        information from a survey that included children in
        the 3rd to 8th grades. The survey covered taste in
        reading, listening to the radio, and the viewing of
        movies.

7.091   Wentroth, Mary Ann. "Public Library Service to
        Children in Oklahoma." Top of the News 31
        (1975):185-191.

        In the state of Oklahoma most of the public
        libraries serve rural communities; thus the state's
        department of libraries has a great impact on local
        services. Staff development, a central resource
        collection and statewide planning of programs are a
        few of the services that the department offers.

7.092   Winnick, Pauline, ed. "Time for Self-Renewal: A
        Special Issue on the Antipoverty Programs." Library
        Journal 91 (1966):317-353.

        Regardless of the good record of traditional
        service, the public library is facing a time of
        self-renewal. Including the undeserved and reaching
        out to the unreached is becoming a part of the
        library scene.

7.093   Wisdom, Elizabeth. "The Development of Good Taste
        in Little Children's Reading." Library Journal 49
        (1924):873-876.

        All children, whether disadvantage or advantage,
        desire good books. Children have a right to explore
        their taste in books as they are directed toward the
        best in literature. Fairytales and books of humor
        feed the imagination, so should be apart of
        childhood reading fare.

7.094   Wolff, Pat. "Read To Me Club." American Libraries
        3 (1972):648-649.

During the summer 1969, the San Bernardino (CA)
County Library System had a "read to me club" for
pre-schoolers. Each pre-school was read ten books,
on which they reported to the librarian. At the end
of the summer, each pre-schooler received a
certificate. What a wonderful way to aid parents in
helping to instill reading interest in their young.

7.095   Yamamoto, M. Catherine. "Junior Great Books
          Discussion Group." Wilson Library Bulletin 34
          (1959):207 and 209.

          The Decatur (IL) Public Library cosponsored with the
          Decatur Public School a Junior Great Books program.
          Good readers who took the SAT in the 5th year of
          school or who were 2 or more grade levels above
          their current grade were invited to participate.
          The response was positive.

8

Story Hour

8.001 Allen, Arthur T. "The Ethos of the Teller of
       Tales." Wilson Library Bulletin 40 (1965):352-355.

       Is there a danger that storytelling will completely
       disappear from one society? In answer to the
       question, the author explores the art of
       storytelling and what makes it special.

8.002 Anderson, Martha Stovicek. "So You Enjoy Telling
       Stories." Library Journal 73 (1948):1059-1062.

       "Hey! I know you. You tell stories." This remark
       greets children's librarians frequently. Anderson
       relates the use of stories in the Whitman County
       (Colfax, WA) District Library, as well as tells the
       story of the survival of the library, itself.

8.003 Baker, Augusta. "How and What to Tell." Library
       Journal 81 (1956):2436-2437.

       Presented is a basic list of books and pamphlets for
       a storyteller.

8.004 Blanchard, Alice A. "Story Telling as a Library
       Tool." Pedogogical Seminary 16 (1909):351-356.

       For publicizing literature, storytelling emerged as
       one of the public library's best employed
       techniques. The goals of children's services in the
       public library was to reach the greatest number of
       children possible, while instilling in them an
       intelligent regard for the best literature; thus
       storytelling accomplished both of the objectives.

8.005   Bowman, James Cloyd. "American Folklore for Boys
          and Girls. Top of the News 6 (December, 1949):20-
          24.

          Folklore is the traditional teachings and wisdom of
          the unlettered elements of society. American folk
          heroes are Paul Bunyan, Pecos Bill, John Henry, Davy
          Crockett, Johnny Appleseed, to name a few. For
          children folklore offers an escape into their
          imagination.

8.006   Britton, Jasmine. "Gudrun Thorne-Thomsen:
          Storyteller from Norway." Horn Book 34 (1958):16-
          28.

          This is a biographical sketch of the life of Gundrun
          Thorne-Thomsen and her many contributions to
          storytelling.

8.007   Burnside, Frances E. "Here's a Story!" Top of the
          News 14 (March, 1958):20-23.

          This is the story of the Jackson (MI) Preschool
          Cooperative Story Hour. Through the cooperative
          efforts of mothers and the library personnel, a
          year-round preschool story hour was presented in
          this library.

8.008   Caples, Beth. "Pre-School Story Hour." Library
          Journal 78 (1953):1805-1808.

          Learning for pre-schoolers should be practical, as
          well as fun. Pre-school story hour at the Enoch
          Pratt Free Library (Baltimore, MD) included picture
          books, music, games and fingerplays.

8.009   Caples, Beth. "The Story Hour." Library Journal 81
          (1956):2012-2014.

          The story hours for three to five year olds are
          important in their own right. Included is a list of
          successful titles used with pre-schoolers. A pre-
          school story hour should combine all the elements of
          learning through play.

8.010   Caples, Beth. "Story Hour for the Three to Five
          Year Olds." Education 75 (1954):155-158.

The author wrote about her preschool story hour as it is conducted at the Central Library of Enoch Pratt Free Library, Baltimore, MD. The response to the story hour has been so positive that no publicity is done.

8.011   Caples, Beth. _Story Hour for the Three to Five Year Old_. Baltimore: Enoch Pratt Free Library, 1953.

Herein is a manual for conducting preschool story hours. Included are a list of stories, records, finger plays, and games to use with three to five year olds.

8.012   Chamberlin, Candace McDowell. "The Preschool Story Hour." _Library Journal_ 69 (1944) 927-928.

Preschool storyhours were educational opportunities for children and parents alike. While the children were being introduced to a group experience and books, their parents were sharing sessions in child guidance and rearing.

8.013   "Children's Issue: Storytelling." _Illinois Libraries_ 51 (1969):1-44.

The theme of this issue comes from the storytelling workshop, which was sponsored by the Children's Services Section of the Illinois Library Association that was held on May 24, 1968, at the University of Illinois/Chicago Circle Campus. The story hour is one of the traditional ways of bringing children and books together.

8.014   "Children's Librarians' Section." _ALA Bulletin_ 3 (1909):408-420.

For this meeting of children's librarians, the format was a symposium on storytelling. Opening the session was a paper by Gudrun Thorne-Thomsen on storytelling in the reading rooms of Chicago's parks. Then storytelling was discussed by representatives of the New York (NY) Public Library, Carnegie Library of Pittsburgh (PA), Brooklyn (NY) Public Library, and Cleveland (OH) Public Library.

8.015   Clarke, Alice W. "The Story Hour." _Library Journal_ 34 (1909):164-165.

In the professional spectrum, there would surface a
variety of views on the nature and composition of
the story hour. For this proponent, the story
hour's purpose should be to stimulate the young to
read. Introduced to children through the story hour
should be literature, relating to nature, history,
and legends.

8.016   Cory, Patricia B. "Library Work with Deaf
         Children." Top of the News 13 (May, 1957):33-36.

         "Out of sight, out of mind" reflects how we view
         deafness. Yet, library work with deaf children is
         very satisfying. Telling stories to deaf children
         requires special effort, but can be done. The
         concrete concepts should be used in stories;
         folklore should not be included.

8.017   Craytor, Hallie Loomis. "Do You Have Stories Here,
         Today?" Wilson Library Bulletin 18 (1943):137-139.

         Preschool storyhours were held in the morning when
         the library was closed to adults. It was a time for
         sharing, telling stories, using poetry, active games
         and drawing.

8.018   Cundriff, Ruby Ethel and Barbara Webb. Story-
         Telling for You: A Handbook of Help for Story-
         Tellers Everywhere. Yellow Springs, OH: The
         Antioch Press, 1957.

         Beginning with the "importance of storytelling,"
         this work then discusses "how to tell stories."

8.019   Dana, John Cotton. "Story-Telling in Libraries."
         Public Libraries 13 (1908):349-351.

         Not all of the professional leaders were avid
         supporters of storytelling as a library technique.
         According to this writer, storytelling belonged in
         the purview of the school as an instructional
         medium.

8.020   Davis, Mary Gould. "The Story-Teller's Art." Horn
         Book 10 (1934):169-175.

Storytelling was one of the "oldest of the arts."
For its power to stimulate our thoughts, to broaden
our horizon, and to offer beauty, the storyteller
should have faith in the tale being told. Marie
Shedlock was cited as having a profound impact on
storytelling.

8.021   De Ronde Edie, Priscilla. "Christmas in the
         Library." Horn Book 21 (1945):434-438.

         Using the Christmas celebration at the 135th Street
         Branch as an example, the children's services of the
         New York (NY) Public Library was portrayed. The
         holiday was a time of new books, story hours and
         reading aloud.

8.022   Draper, Aimee F. "By Appointment." Horn Book 25
         (1949):551-554.

         Pre-school Story Hour at the Patterham Branch of the
         Public Library of Brookline, MA was by appointment.
         It was held for the general public and nursery
         schools by appointment.

8.023   Duff, Ida J. "Storytelling in the Brooklyn Public
         Library." ALA Bulletin 3 (1909):415-417.

         Programming at the Brooklyn (NY) Public Library was
         adapted to the particular needs and circumstances of
         each branch. Although there had been some positive
         results from storytelling, not all branches saw the
         benefits of having a regular story hour.

8.024   Edwin, Natalie Mayo. "Anyone Can Tell Stories."
         Wilson Library Bulletin 34 (1960):658-660.

         Anyone can tell stories if the person really wishes
         to tell them and is willing to spend the necessary
         time on the process. This article deals with
         selection, preparation, and delivery.

8.025   Elsmo, Nancy. "Infants and Toddlers Have a Right to
         be Read to: Reading Aloud - How to Start and Keep
         Going." Wisconsin Library Bulletin 68 (1972):285-
         287+.

         It is not too early to start reading aloud to
         children, when they are in the cradle. For the

development of language skills and reading
readiness, infants should be exposed to reading
aloud.

8.026   Engler, Martha C. "Message Versus Machine: The Art
          of the Storyteller." Catholic Library World 44
          (1973):471-477.

          Even though machines are popular with children, the
          art of the storyteller should still be practiced.
          Through storytelling all humankind has a common
          bond.

8.027   Escalante, Hildamar. "Story-Telling Around the
          World: A Symposium, Part V: South America."
          Library Journal 65 (1940):624-627.

          For the people of Latin America, storytelling was a
          normal part of life. Stories were apart of the
          common thread of life that went on generation to
          generation. Most storytelling took place in the
          home.

8.028   Fannin, Gwendolyn Marie. "A Resume of the History,
          Growth and Development of the Story Hour in the New
          York Public Library." MSLS Thesis, Atlanta
          University, 1958.

          The story hour at the New York (NY) Public Library
          was the focus of this study. Here, story hours
          originated; and the process became a model in
          children's librarianship.

8.029   Federgren, Dorothea. "The Preschool Story Hour."
          Illinois Libraries 43 (1961):505-510.

          The rationale for a preschool story hour is
          presented. Then the how of storytelling for
          preschoolers is discussed, along with the
          frustrations in the process. At the end, are lists
          of successful picture books and folktales for the
          preschool story hour.

8.030   Frishman, Nettie. "Storytelling Festival in Topanga
          Plaza." Top of the News 26 (1970):294-296.

          For National Library Week, the West Valley (CA)
          Library had a storytelling festival in a shopping

plaza. The shopping center provided a tent, folding
chairs, and lighting while the library supplied the
manpower - 15 children's librarians. Over 1400
children, ranging in age from 3 to 14 were reached.

8.031   Fritz, Jean. "Two-way Story Hours." Library
Journal 79 (1954):1372-1374.

Children should be given an opportunity to
participate, as well as, listen in story hours. To
have participation, the story hour became the "Magic
Carpet Club" for 5 to 8 year olds. The children
responded well to the format.

8.032   Gallagher, Anne and Eugene Irving. "Once Upon a
Time . . ." Illinois Libraries 57 (1975):325-328.

Starting in 1969, there was conducted a special
story hour for five and six year olds at the public
library. Included were stories, finger plays,
creative dramatics, games and the idea of writing a
story.

8.033   Godley, Margaret. "Once Upon a Time . . ." Wilson
Library Bulletin 30 (1955):530-531.

For interested adults from all walks of life, the
Savannah (GA) Public Library held an institute on
storytelling. Ruth Theobald Young of Frankfort,
Kentucky was the instructor. A general overview of
the event is presented.

8.034   Greene, Ellin. "The Preschool Story Hour Today."
Top of the News 31 (1974):80-85.

A preschool story hour should be library-centered
whether using books, films, filmstrips or records.
The preschool story hour should provide the
preschooler with opportunities for listening,
looking, and selecting media for home use. Pointers
for effective preschool sessions are included.

8.035   Gwin, Edna H. "Story Hour Becomes an Asset."
Wilson Library Bulletin 18 (1944):678-679.

Varying the format of the story hour proved to be a
very positive happening. The chief technique was

through dramatization. Included are a list of
stories that lend themselves to dramatic play.

8.036   Gymer, Rose C. "Storytelling in the Cleveland
        Public Library." ALA Bulletin 3 (1909):417-420.

        Serving as the rationale for storytelling were 1)
        the fact that it was a means of directing and
        stimulating juvenile readers and 2) that it served
        as a medium for difficult materials. Storytelling
        was an effective way of reaching a large number of
        children through one endeavor. Examples of what
        impact story hours were having were also discussed.

8.037   Hamilton, Ruth Hewitt. "'From Drawbridge to Castle'
        - Stories Reign Supreme." Library Journal 81
        (1956):2016-2018.

        Through story hours, the librarian has the
        opportunity to meet with children in a relaxed and
        intimate manner. The story hour is free of
        competition or hidden motives. Its sole
        justification is that the personal sharing of the
        magic appeal of a good story is an exciting and
        rewarding experience.

8.038   Hassler, Harriot E. "Common Sense and the Story
        Hour." Library Journal 30 (1905):c76-78.

        The aim for all storytelling should be the
        improvement of juvenile reading. Not only should
        children be introduced to good literature via the
        story hour, but they should be stimulated to expand
        their interest in the realm of non-fiction.

8.039   Hazeltine, A. I. "Storytelling in the Carnegie
        Library of Pittsburgh." ALA Bulletin 3 (1909):413-
        415.

        For the Carnegie Library of Pittsburgh, the story
        hour provided a platform for giving the right book
        to the right child at the right time. Through this
        vehicle, the relationship between the librarian and
        the child was cemented; a positive attitude was
        fostered about the library; listening skills were
        developed; and children were introduced to an array
        of great literature.

8.040   Hill, Ruth A. "Story-Telling Around the World: A
          Symposium, Part I: United States." Library Journal
          65 (1940):285-289.

          Opening with the historical perspective of the art
          of storytelling, this paper represented the survey
          of story hours on the American scene. Given were
          the purposes of storytelling, types of stories, and
          the training, which was required.

8.041   Hitchcock, Olga Mary. "Radio Adventures in Books."
          Wilson Library Bulletin 18 (1944):674-675.

          Since July, 1942, the Lincoln (NE) City Library did
          a story hour on the radio, "Adventures in Books."
          It was fifteen minutes, which featured six to eight
          books that related to stories or hobbies. Over the
          years, dramatization and junior book reviewers were
          used in the series.

8.042   Huls, Ardis. "Preschool Story Hour." Wilson
          Library Bulletin 16 (1942):726-727 and 730.

          In this account, the development of a preschool
          story hour series was discussed. In the beginning
          the children were given time to browse through
          books, then two stories were told. As the series
          went on other facets were added.

8.043   Izard, Anne. "The Pleasure is Mutural: A Report to
          the Profession." Top of the News 23 (1967):371-375.

          Out of a professional dream came the idea of a film
          to teach the rudiments of preschool story hour to
          volunteers and students. In this report is a
          detailed account of how the film, "The Pleasure is
          Mutual," came to be made.

8.044   Jordan, Alice M. "Story-Telling in Boston." Horn
          Book 10 (1934):177-184.

          In 1904, Marie Shedlock presented the first story
          hour at the Boston (MA) Public Library. No longer
          an experiment, this method of opening books to
          children has become increasingly important through
          the years. In Boston, the story hours were
          conducted, at that time, by the Cronans and Mrs.
          Powers.

8.045   Joyce, Donald F.   "Project OBAC: To Tell a Black
          Child a Story." Illinois Libraries 54 (1972):203-
          204.

          Addressing the request by a black librarian for
          material for black children, a group of young black
          writers in Chicago, developed a special series of
          story hours for children. There was a preschool
          hour for younger children and a regular story hour
          for school age children.

8.046   Karrick, Ethel C. "The Preschool Story Hour." ALA
          Bulletin 41 (1947):445-448.

          Introducing children to the library and books was
          the chief goal of children's librarianship. Using
          the preschool story hour as a medium for that goal
          was a positive opportunity in children's services.
          This article presented the guidelines for a
          preschool story hour and its rationale.

8.047   Kimmel, Eric A. "Starting in Storytelling."
          Elementary English 51 (1974):559-560.

          Codifying storytelling into eight categories the
          author presents what a beginning storyteller needs
          to know to undertake the art.

8.048   Kimmel, Margaret Mary. "Stair-Step Stories." Top
          of the News. 23 (1967):154-156.

          Working with the Baltimore Urban Renewal and Housing
          Agency (BURHA), two children's librarians at the
          Enoch Pratt Free Library (Baltimore, MD) did a
          summer session of storytelling on the steps of a
          home in a block of the city. Used in the sessions
          were picture books and folklore.

8.049   Kircher, Clara J. "Children and Parents Go to
          'School'." Wilson Library Bulletin 29 (1954):155-
          160.

          This was a thorough presentation of how preschool
          story hours were conducted in the Newark (NJ) Public
          Library. For the young preschoolers, going to story
          hour was equated with going to school.

8.050   Kohberger, Kathryn. "Let's Tell a Story." Wilson
         Library Bulletin 21 (1946):158-159.

         The Carnegie Library of Pittsburgh started a radio
         program, "Let's Tell a Story," for the primary
         grades in the city's school system. Each session
         was taped before a class in a different school each
         week. After conducting the series for awhile, the
         library did a survey of its work and was pleased
         with the findings.

8.051   Komor, Judith. "What Makes a Story Good to Tell?"
         Top of the News 19 (March, 1963):65-68.

         In the storytelling process, there are two factors -
         the storyteller and the story. The main component
         is the story. The storyteller is the medium through
         which the story is imparted. A good story has
         simple language and is built around a unifying idea
         or plot.

8.052   Larrick, Nancy. "Poetry in the Story Hour." Top of
         the News 32 (1976):151:161.

         Using poetry in a story hour can turn it into a
         poetry happening. Not only does poetry in the story
         hour allow for group participation, it can be
         interpreted through a number of performing arts and
         media.

8.053   Lyman, Edna. "The Story Hour." Wisconsin Library
         Bulletin 1 (1905):4-6.

         Sharing the story hour experience was an opportunity
         for cultivating a positive interest in quality
         literature. Presented was the program of the
         Pittsburgh library as an excellent example of
         material for the story hour series.

8.054   Lyman, Edna. Story Telling: What to Tell and How
         to Tell it. Chicago: A. C. McClurg and Co., 1923.

         Paying tribute to the revival of storytelling as an
         art, this handbook served as a resource tool for the
         beginning storyteller. Opening with the social
         objective of books, the work proceeded to discuss
         the techniques of reading aloud and storytelling, as
         well as contained an overview of the various types
         of oral literature to be shared with children.

8.055   McConnell, Ruth and Frances Postell. "Books for
        Roosevelt Grady." Library Journal 89 (1964):3384-
        3386.

        The counties of Multnomah, Clackamas, and Washington
        in the state of Oregon did a volunteer program for
        migrant children in their communities. They made
        twenty-five visits to six camps in the area from
        late June through early August. The volunteer
        venture was a success, telling stories and leading
        to books.

8.056   Masel, Arlene. "Tell Me Another." Wilson Library
        Bulletin 35 (1960):129-144.

        Presented is a list of annotated stories by month.
        The list is for storytellers, teachers and
        librarians. Each month has about 20 suggestions,
        which were selected with a view to holidays, weather
        or special occasions.

8.057   Mathy, Margaret. "Folklore and Flapjacks Family
        Style." Top of the News 28 (1972):198-201.

        The Children's Department of the Dayton and
        Montgomery County (OH) Public Library presented a
        Sunday morning story time on the radio as a public
        services presentation. During the fifteen minutes
        stories were shared, as well as poetry and music.

8.058   Moore, Anne Carroll. "Our Fairy Godmother: Marie
        L. Shedlock." Horn Book 10 (1934):136-143.

        Marie L. Shedlock was brought to the attention of
        the library profession by Mary Wright Plummer.
        Plummer invited her to tell stories at the Pratt
        Institute for the faculty, students, and assistants;
        then Shedlock visited and told stories at libraries
        in America. Shedlock was credited for bringing a
        lasting respect for the art of storytelling to
        America.

8.059   Moore, Annie Carroll. "Report on Storytelling."
        Library Journal 35 (1910):404-412.

        The report of the Committee on Storytelling opened
        by citing the impact of Marie L. Shedlock as a
        storyteller. Then information which was gleaned
        from a survey made of storytelling in thirteen
        cities was presented.

8.060   Moore, Annie Carroll. "The Story Hour at Pratt
          Institute Free Library." Library Journal 30
          (1905):204-211.

          Under the rubric of the story hour, the Pratt
          Institute Free Library developed a literature
          series. Using not only storytelling, but reading-
          aloud and lectures, a corps of individuals were
          presented in the evening series. During the year,
          special holidays, celebrations, and themes were
          highlighted.

8.061   Moore, Annie Carroll. "Story-Telling in the New
          York Public Library." ALA Bulletin 3 (1909):410-
          413.

          For many professionals, storytelling was considered
          an art that was the best medium of expression for
          revealing quality literature to children. In the
          New York (NY) Public Library it was seen as a method
          of raising the whole tone of the work for children
          in a library. This discussion followed the
          development of the story hour at the New York Public
          Library.

8.062   Moore, Vardine, Pre-School Story Hour. Metuchen,
          NJ: The Scarecrow Press, Inc., 1966.

          Preschoolers as an age group are valued and
          cherished patrons of the public library. The
          preschool story hour has become an important facet
          of children's librarianship. This work is the "how
          to" of preschool programming.

8.063   "The Musical Story Hour During Vacation." Wisconsin
          Library Bulletin 23 (1927):150-151.

          During the summer, a story hour series was conducted
          using composers and their music. Not only music,
          but biography and poetry were included.

8.064   Nesbitt, Elizabeth. "The Art of Storytelling."
          Catholic Library World 34 (1962):143-145+.

          The unique function of children's work is to give to
          children the joy of reading. Among the methods of
          reading guidance, there is storytelling for group
          work. It is the only reading guidance method which
          recreates the literature with which it is concerned.

8.065   Nesbitt, Elizabeth. "The Art of Storytelling."
          Horn Book 21 (1945):439-444.

          Sharing stories was apart of all cultures. Most
          folk literature, whether folktale, legends, myth, or
          epic, was in the oral tradition in the beginning.
          It was humankind's way of explaining the unknown and
          inculcating a value system.

8.066   Nesbitt, Elizabeth. "Hold to that Which is Good."
          Horn Book 16 (1940):7-15.

          For children's service, the supreme purpose was to
          introduce literature to children. The most
          effective means to that end was storytelling. The
          purpose of library storytelling was to cultivate the
          capacity for literary appreciation in children.

8.067   Nesbitt, Elizabeth. "Storytelling - The Creative
          Way." Catholic Library World 36 (1964):230-232.

          ". . . The arts are probably the strongest and
          deepest of all educative forces." Storytelling is
          such an art, a strong and deep educative force
          because it wears the warmth and color of the senses.

8.068   Nowlin, Clifford H. The Story Teller and His Pack.
          Springfield, MA: Milton Bradley Co., 1929.

          This manual on storytelling was developed as an
          instructional tool for the profession. Covered was
          the historical perspective, the objectives of the
          process, the acquisition of the art of storytelling,
          its employment in the educational sector, and
          discussions of various types of oral literature.

8.069   Olcott, Frances J. "Storytelling: A Public Library
          Method." Pedagogical Seminary 16 (1909):545-547.

          Since the public library was a popular educational
          development, it supplemented the work of the church,
          the home, the school, and the kindergarten. Its
          function was to place within the reach of all the
          best thought of the world as reflected in the
          printed page. To this end, storytelling was used to
          introduce a mass of children simultaneously to great
          literature.

8.070   Olcott, Frances J. "Storytelling as a Means of
          Teaching Literature." New York Libraries 4
          (1914):38-45.

          Opening with the discussion of the universality of
          the oral tradition, therein was traced the antiquity
          of the folk art. Storytelling proved to be an
          effective technique for sharing all types of
          literature with children whether in the home, the
          school, or the public library.

8.071   Peterson, Ellin F. "The Pre-School Hour." Top of
          the News 18 (December, 1961):47-51.

          The Pre-school Hour in the public library is an
          outgrowth of the interests in child development and
          early childhood education. It is a library book-
          centered program, which has its own set of goals and
          objectives.

8.072   Pfaender, Ann McLelland and Eloise West Winstedt.
          "Story-Telling Around the World: A Symposium, Part
          IV: Hawaii." Library Journal 65 (1940):574-577.

          The storytelling in the Islands was dominated by the
          cultural diversity that existed there. The legends
          of ancient Hawaii were always well-received. In
          most cases, the story hours were conducted in the
          schools or on Saturdays.

8.073   Quigley, Mary G. "Telling Stories to Children."
          Public Libraries 10 (1905):351-353.

          Serving as the primary objectives of storytelling
          should be: 1) the development of the imagination,
          2) the cultivation of a taste for good literature,
          and 3) the establishment of a conduit to the whole
          array of reading matter. Then presented were the
          fundamentals of storytelling.

8.074   Rollins, Charlemae. "Storytelling." Illinois
          Libraries 42 (1960):134-137.

          "Please tell us a story": is a request that
          librarians receive. There will be many
          opportunities to tell stories. Given is the formula
          for good storytelling.

8.075   Sanborn, Florence.   "How to Use Picture-Story
         Books." Library Journal 74 (1949):272-274.

         With the increase of publishing of picture books, a
         new source of materials was provided for
         storytelling. How to effectively use the picture
         book in storytelling sessions was the object of this
         article.

8.076   Schoenfeld, Madalynne.   "A Children's Theater in
         Yonkers." Wilson Library Bulletin 40 (1965):352-
         355.

         The Sprain Brook Theatre was sponsored by the
         Children's Department of the Yonkers (NY) Public
         Library. With limited opportunity for access to the
         theatre, the library decided to present productions
         for its juvenile patrons.

8.077   Sell, Violet.   "Not Some Day, But Now!" Wilson
         Library Bulletin 25 (1951):674-675.

         After talking about the benefits and joys of
         presenting a preschool story hour and mother's
         discussion group, the librarians at the North Long
         Beach Branch, Long Beach (CA) Public Library made it
         a reality. Starting with a preschool story hour,
         the need naturally evolved for an adult discussion
         group.

8.078   Shedlock, Marie L.   The Art of the Story-Teller.
         Foreword by Anne Carroll Moore.   Third Edition,
         Revised. New York: Dover Publications, Inc., 1951.

         Considered the seminal work on storytelling, this
         resource conveyed the wisdom and perspectives of
         Shedlock, who was an advocate for storytelling in
         public librarianship. In part two of the work,
         there are the stories for which the artist was well-
         known. This work was originally published in 1915
         by S. Appleton - Century Century, Inc.

8.079   Sheehan, Ethna.   "Story-Telling is Fun." Library
         Journal 77 (1952):675-679.

         Discussed are the many facets of storytelling.
         Basically, the article is aimed at the neophytes of
         the storytelling art.

8.080   Sheviak, Margaret R.   "Creative Dance Group Enlivens
          Summer Reading Program." Library Journal 84
          (1959):1304-1305.

          At the Louisville (KY) Free Public Library, dancing
          was integrated into the regular summer story hour.
          As the storyteller told the story, a dance group did
          an interpretation of it.

8.081   Sivertz, Chloe T.   "Back Yard Storytelling." Wilson
          Library Bulletin 12 (1949):624-625, 628.

          Through the activity of the Friends of the Seattle
          (WA) Public Library, an unique project was developed
          for mothers. They became storytellers in their
          backyards. So successful was the project that it
          expanded to include creative dramatics and puppetry.

8.082   Smith, William Jay. "Rhythm of the Night:
          Reflections on Reading Aloud to Children." Horn
          Book 36 (1960):495-500.

          Author and poet, William Jay Smith reflects on the
          impact and power of reading aloud to his sons.

8.083   Steese, Laura M.   "Parents, Children, and the
          Library." Wilson Library Bulletin 20 (1945):215-
          217.

          This was an account of a successful preschool story
          hour and parents' group. In the story hour a
          variety of media and techniques were used. The
          parents' group grew out of a desire for more
          understanding of childhood and what they could bring
          to it.

8.084   Steinmetz, Eulalie M.   "Storytelling in the New York
          Public Library." Top of the News 5 (May, 1949):6-8.

          In the New York (NY) Public Library, story hours are
          held from Halloween to the festival of May Day on a
          weekly bases. Discussed is the how of storytelling
          as it is manifested in the New York Public Library.

8.085   Taylor, Virginia. "Story-Telling." Top of the News
          24 (1967) 8-10.

Believing in active participation by the children, Taylor used storytelling to elicit a positive reaction from Spanish-speaking children. After telling "The Three Billy Goats Gruff," the juvenile audience told similar tales from their Spanish culture.

8.086   Tone, Mary. "Preschool Story Programs" Library Journal 78 (1953):673-674.

Responding to the newest group of patrons of the Gary (IN) Public Library, there was developed a series of preschool story hours. The programs were held at 10:30 a.m. in the morning. Each series ran for ten weeks: February to April, July to August, and September to November. Included in the program were picture books, records, and games.

8.087   Tooze, Ruth. Storytelling. Englewood Cliffs, NJ: Prentice-Hall, Inc., 1959.

Storytelling is an art, which can be practiced by all who work with children. Through storytelling children and young people are taught and entertained. Not only does the work deal with the fundamentals of storytelling, there is an extensive bibliography for the storyteller's use.

8.088   Trotter, Frances W. "Story-Telling Around the World: A Symposium, Part III: Canada." Library Journal 65 (1940):484-487.

As the country had many physical faces, its wealth of stories was vast, beginning with Indian legends. In the various provinces, each public library system followed different pattern, from telling stories at special times to having regular story hours.

8.089   Tucker, Harold W. "Operation Head Start." Library Journal 89 (1964):3382-3383.

The Queens Borough (NY) Public Library conducted a reading readiness program in ten branches in the city that served disadvantaged neighborhoods. The objectives of the project were to conduct weekly preschool story hours, to run a series of adult education to assure carry-over into the home and to encourage the development of home libraries.

8.090   Uebelacker, Susan. "Story Hour for the Blind." <u>Top</u>
          <u>of</u> <u>the</u> <u>News</u> 22 (1966):414-417.

          Having a special series of story hours for the blind
          children, required planning. The story hour
          included sighted children, as well. For the story
          hour short stories should be told, using jokes,
          riddles, and simple stand-up exercises as pace
          breakers.

8.091   Viguers, Ruth Hill. "Over the Drawbridge and into
          the Castle." <u>Horn</u> <u>Book</u> 27 (1951):54-62.

          Opening with a picture of the ancient troubadour,
          Viguers painted a history of the various
          storytellers through the ages. Then the article
          chronicled the joys of storytelling on the library
          scene, where the children's librarian reaped the
          best of the past.

8.092   Wessel, Miriam A. "The Story Hour Program in the
          Public Library." <u>Top</u> <u>of</u> <u>the</u> <u>News</u> 11 (April,
          1955):11-15.

          The story hour program has had a long and continuous
          history in children's librarianship. Presented in
          this article are the techniques for such
          programming.

8.093   White, Pura Belpre. "A Bilingual Story Hour
          Program." <u>Library</u> <u>Journal</u> 89 (1964):3379-3381.

          At the 115th Street branch of the New York (NY)
          Public Library, a bilingual program of children's
          services was adopted. Storytelling, poetry, and
          puppetry were utilized in the bilingual programming.

8.094   Ziskind, Sylvia. <u>Telling</u> <u>Stories</u> <u>to</u> <u>Children</u>. New
          York: The H. W. Wilson Company, 1976.

          This is a practical handbook on the mechanics of
          storytelling and creative dramatics. It is a
          resource for the inexperienced and experienced
          storyteller.

9

Interagency Cooperation

9.001   Adams, C. F. "Public Library and Schools." Library
         Journal 1 (1876):437-441.

         Adams believed that if the public library was to be
         a successful adjunct to the public school, it had a
         responsibility for nurturing the reading interests
         of juveniles. Each agency should share in the
         obligation of introducing children to literature in
         order to cultivate a love for good reading.

9.002   Bard, Harriet E. "Reaching the Unreached."
         Wisconsin Library Bulletin 62 (1966):7-15.

         Richmond, Indiana's Morrisson-Reeves Library
         developed two outreach programs. Libraries were
         opened for the Boy's Club and in the Townsend
         Community Center.

9.003   Barette, Emma E. "Use of the Library as Aids in
         School - Room Work." School and Society 7
         (1918):309-312.

         Challenging students to extend their studies beyond
         the textbook could be accomplished through a weekly
         planned project, which utilized library research.
         Students should investigate a topic of their choice
         in various reference sources, presenting their
         findings to the class.

9.004   Batchelder, Mildred L. "What Librarians are Doing
         or Can Do." ALA Bulletin 38 (1944):27 and 31.

         Librarians were encouraged to participate in
         community service organizations. It was suggested

that they work with other adults who had a concern
for the young. Work for the advancement of the
young through resources and programming was
suggested.

9.005   Bates, Henry E. "Jitney Library Service." Illinois
        Libraries (1972):279-283.

        In early 1969, the Douglass Branch of the Chicago
        (IL) Public Library started a program of bussing
        classes from eight elementary schools to the
        library. The sessions were conducted by library
        assistants, using all types of media.

9.006   Bean, Mary A. "Report on the Reading of the Young."
        Library Journal (1883):217-227.

        This was the second annual report on the reading of
        the young. A survey was made of all the major
        libraries to glean what work was being done. Most
        of the activities included cooperation with public
        schools.

9.007   Beik, Doris Humphrey. "A Girl Scout Program."
        Wilson Library Bulletin 15 (1941):498-499.

        Working with the Girl Scouts brought the librarian
        in contact with children of all ages and adults, as
        well. Presented were a variety of opportunities for
        being of service to that group.

9.008   Bennett, Adelaide. "The School Department of the
        Denver Public Library." Library Journal 64
        (1939):91-94.

        An overview of the work, as well as a special study
        by the school department of the Denver (CO) Public
        Library was presented. Not only did they supply
        classroom collections to the schools of the city,
        the department held a large picture file, from which
        teachers could withdraw items.

9.009   Birtwell, C. W. "Home Libraries." Library Journal
        29 (1894):9-13.

        Birtwell started the project of "home libraries" in
        Boston, MA, as a part of the services of the
        Children's Aid Society. Presented was a detailed

account of the home libraries and how the project functioned.

9.010   Bishop, William W. "Training in the Use of Books."
          The Sewanee Review 20 (1912):265-281.

          To set the stage for the discussion of training, an
          overview was presented on the growth of publishing.
          Because of the importance of books in learning,
          every child should be trained in bibliographic
          instruction, starting with elementary school.
          Therein was presented a program for such instruction
          at both the elementary and secondary levels of
          education.

9.011   Bostwick, Arthur, ed. The Relationship Between the
          Library and the Public Schools. New York: The H.
          W. Wilson Company, 1914.

          This volume in a series on Classic of American
          Librarianship was devoted to interagency cooperation
          between the public library and the public schools.
          The earliest article was by Charles Francis Adams,
          Jr., which was published in 1876 in Library Journal
          and titled "The Public Library and the Public
          School." It was the first call for cooperation
          between these two social institutions.

9.012   Burke, T. Gordon and Gerald R. Shields, Editors.
          Children's Library Service: School or Public?
          Metuchen, NJ: The Scarecrow Press, Inc., 1974.

          Contained herein are the recommendations of the
          state of New York's Report of the Commissioner of
          Education's Committee on Library Development 1970.
          Along with the recommendations, are various
          reactions to the report by school and public
          librarians.

9.013   Chamberlain, Mellen. "Public Library and Public
          School." Library Journal 5 (1880):299-302.

          The chief functions of the public library are to
          answer inquiries, to supply suitable reading for
          all, and to instruct the students in public schools.
          The last function served as the objective for a
          special project with a school, which was conducted
          by the Boston (MA) Public Library.

9.014   "Children's Book Week in Libraries" Library Journal
           45 (1920):835-838.

           Functioning as catalysis for the development of the
           observance of "Children's Book Week" were the New
           York area public libraries and the major publisher
           therein. New York City was seen as the largest
           center for book distribution in the country and
           charged itself with sitting the stage for the
           national celebration of Children's Book Week. To
           this end, every agency which was involved with the
           young was solicited for support to make this
           celebration as successful venture.

9.015   Clark, George T. "Methods of School Circulation of
           Library Books." Library Journal 31 (1905):155-157.

           There are three methods for providing books to
           schools, which are 1) students borrowing them, 2)
           the use of teachers' card, and 3) classroom
           collections. For public libraries, the most
           effective was the program of classroom collections,
           which provided service to the greater number of
           students.

9.016   Clasen, Robert E. and Donald M. Miller. "Project
           Head Start and the Library." Wisconsin Library
           Bulletin 62 (1966):1-6.

           An overview is presented of the Head Start project.
           Then the Madison, WI program is discussed, along
           with the library's involvement.

9.017   Cowing, Agnes. "Some Experiments in Work with
           Elementary School Children." Library Journal 43
           (1918):210-214.

           Work with seventh and eight grade pupils was
           discussed. Using the time period in the school for
           library hour, the children's librarian presented
           book-talks, coupling the techniques of storytelling
           and reading aloud.

9.018   Cox, Mary Frances. "Team Work." Wilson Library
           Bulletin 20 (1945):148-149.

           Cooperation was a word that represented working
           together for a common good. In Atlanta, the public
           school, the public library and Rich's department
           store worked together on a summer project, which

took storytelling to the children in the city and
county, served by the public library.

9.019   Darling, Richard L.   "4-H Clubs and Libraries:
         Conference Report."   Top of the News (1965):359-361.

         Six state and national 4-H club leaders, along with
         five librarians who represented children's and young
         adult librarians met at the National 4-H Center in
         Chevy Chase, Maryland. The purpose was to explore
         how the two agencies might be more involved in
         cooperative endeavors. Used as a context for the
         discussion was the Kansas project between libraries
         and 4-H clubs.

9.020   Dewey, Mevil.   "Relation of School Libraries to the
         Public Library System."   Public Libraries 10
         (1905):224-225.

         Discussing the controversy of who should have
         authority for school libraries, Dewey stated that
         these departments could be more efficient under the
         aegis of the public library. Cited as compelling
         reasons were: 1) the public libraries capacity to
         facilitate all facets of library services, and 2)
         the more positive role of the public librarian as a
         reading advocate.

9.021   Doren, Electra Collins.   "The Library and the
         School: Work Now Done."   Library Journal 29
         (1904):153-157.

         Using the survey method, analysis was made of the
         status and extent of services that public libraries
         were providing schools. The two broad categories
         were distribution which included classroom
         collections, deposit stations, and teachers and
         reference services. Gleaned also, were the
         operational principles for this phase of children's
         work.

9.022   Downey, Mary Elizabeth.   "Relation of the Public
         Schools to the Various Library Agencies."   Library
         Journal 45 (1920):883-886.

         Within the educational process, the function of the
         librarian should be to instill the reading habit in
         students, as well as to teach independent library
         use. Outlined was the role of the teacher and the

librarian, along with a discussion of each
institutional commitment to the process.

9.023   Dowsman, Mary E. "Books for the Play Ground."
        Wisconsin Library Bulletin 3 (1907):83-84.

        Through its extension services, the Milwaukee (WI)
        Public Library established a playground library
        during the summer in a distant neighborhood from a
        regular library outlet. Using children's service as
        the channel into the unreached community proved such
        a successful project that the resources were
        relocated to a settlement house in the area.

9.024   Eastman, Charlotte Whitney. "Educational Ideals in
        School and Library." Iowa Library Quarterly 3
        (1903):25-28.

        The ideal conviction for the school and the library
        would be that the individually of the child was the
        governing facet in the reading habit. Not only was
        the school and library important, but the home
        situation was a factor to be considered.

9.025   Eastman, Linda A. "The Child, the School and the
        Library." Library Journal 21 (1896):134-139.

        From the school, the child receives the skills and
        tools for learning, while in the library the child
        applies these. Library instruction should be
        integrated into all of the courses of study in a
        school situation.

9.026   Elmendorf, Henry L. "The School Department of the
        Buffalo Public Library." Library Journal 28
        (1903):157-160.

        Through the schools, the library was able to reach
        the largest body of citizens in the most effective
        manner. This objective had favorable impact on
        fostering school/library cooperation. Discussed was
        the practice of the Buffalo Public Library with the
        city's schools.

9.027   Foster, W. E. "The Relation of the Libraries to the
        School System." Library Journal 5 (1880):99-104.

Presented in this discussion was the role of the
public library in the instructional program of the
community. Not only was the public library seen as
holding a valuable collection of materials, but as a
very important operative in the educational process
from the primary grades through the secondary level
of training.

9.028   Foster, W. E. "School and the Library: Their
         Mutual Relation." Library Journal 4 (1879):319-325.

         Having the same basic purposes, the school and the
         public library were united as operatives for
         supplying information to the community and for
         providing instruction. Although their contact
         points were different, the two should develop
         methods of cooperation which would enhance the
         instructional process in the young.

9.029   Gatch, Ruth Gordon. "Relation of the Parent and
         Librarian to Children's Reading." Iowa Library
         Quarterly 5 (1907):175-177.

         Not only should the parent read with the child, but
         should read the books that their child reads. In
         the home, reading should be a daily practice.
         Parents were apt to be careless with the mental fare
         of their children.

9.030   Green, Samuel S. "The Relation of the Public
         Library to the Public Schools." Library Journal 5
         (1880):235-245.

         Relating the ways in which the Worcester (MA) Public
         Library worked with the local institutions of
         instruction, the librarian discussed a special
         project, which was designed for the seventh, eighth,
         and ninth grades. Using geography as the focus for
         the project, a special demonstration was developed
         for instructors, then used to initiate the
         undertaking.

9.031   Hallock, Arthur C. K. and Beatrice S. Stone.
         "Children in a Democracy." ALA Bulletin 36
         (1942):404-407.

         "Children in a democracy" was the theme for the
         fourth White House Conference on children. Although
         ideas on child welfare and needed services
         originated at the conference, each state was

required to supply the necessary follow-up, then was
presented the library's role in the state of
Massachusetts.

9.032   Hardman, Elizabeth. "Helping Children Know Library
        Tools." Public Libraries 12 (1907):299-301.

        Working with a topic of interest, a reference
        presentation was made for classes in the eighth and
        ninth grades by the librarian. During each session,
        the pupils were introduced to the major resources in
        that subject area.

9.033   Hartt, Mary Bronson. "Children's Museums." Outlook
        111 (1915):673-677.

        Expanding the realm of nature studies and serving as
        a conduit to broader cultural horizons, were the
        fundamental principles of museums that were
        especially designed for children or children's
        departments in such institutions. In an informal
        atmosphere, the young should encounter the wonders
        of the world.

9.034   Hazeltine, Alice I. "The St. Louis Teachers Room."
        Public Libraries 24 (1919):368-369.

        Opened by the public library was a room, especially
        for teachers. In it was a small pedagogical
        collection of books. Special classes in instruction
        were presented for educators at the public library.

9.035   Herbert, Clara W. "Establishing Relations Between
        the Children's Library and Other Civic Agencies."
        Library Journal 34 (1909):195-196.

        Cited were the two purposes of children's services
        in the public library. The first and foremost
        should be to reach directly with the services of the
        public library as many children, as possible. To
        this should be the establishment of a cooperative
        relationship with all agencies that rendered
        services to the young.

9.036   Hewins, C. M. "Yearly Report on Boys' and Girls'
        Reading." Library Journal 7 (1882):182-190.

In March, 1882, Hewins sent out cards to the
librarians of the twenty-five leading libraries in
the country, to inquire what were they doing for
juvenile reading. Most of the replies focused on
work with schools.

9.037   Hunt, Clara W. "Arousing an Interest in the Great
         Classics for Children." New York Libraries 3
         (1912):47-51.

         Although children read the mediocre books, it was
         the responsibility of the teacher and librarian to
         introduce them to the classics. Teachers had a
         special influence on their pupils and through their
         enthusiasm had created a demand for a given title
         that impacted on the library.

9.038   James, Hannah P. "Yearly Report on the Reading of
         the Young." Library Journal 10 (1885):278-291.

         Surveys were sent to 125 public libraries and 75
         responses were returned. Work with schools was the
         most important facet for reaching young people.

9.039   Johnson, Siddie Joe. "The Children's Room and the
         Community." Library Journal 66 (1941):763-767.

         Through the activities of the Children's Room, an
         array of agencies in the community met. Industry,
         commerce, education, amusement and child welfare
         services had been integrated in the happenings of
         children's work.

9.040   Judd, Charles H. "The Library and the School." ALA
         Bulletin 4 (1910):607-611.

         From the perspective of an educator, an assessment
         was made of an approach to interagency cooperation.
         The study hour was seen as a time to expose the
         pupils to a wide array of books that enhanced their
         course work. Working with small groups of students,
         the public librarian became an operative for the
         students exposure to other resources that expanded
         their educational horizon.

9.041   Kent, Henry W. "Cooperation Between Libraries,
         Schools and Museums." Library Journal (1911):557-
         560.

Through a cooperative mode, the work of the public
library, the school, and the museum should be
integrated. Through the museum, the educational
studies and the reading of books were expanded and
illuminated by the visual presentations in the
exhibits.

9.042   Kerr, Willis H. "What May the Library Do for the
School? Library Journal 41 (1916):34-36.

Accepting the library as a positive component of the
educational process, it was perceived as a great
composite textbook, which served to foster natural
interests and to address real problems of students.
So important was the library in the instructional
scheme that it should be a part of every school
structure, starting with the primary level.

9.043   Latimer, Louise P. "School Work of the Public
Library of the District of Columbia." Library
Journal 42 (1917):715-718.

Presented was an account of the school work in the
DCPL. Through the school department of the public
library, it had reached 115 grade schools in the
area with only a central agency and one branch.

9.044   Lenroot, Katharine F. "The Children's Bureau and
Libraries." ALA Bulletin 38 (1944):26-27.

The Children's Bureau of the U.S. Dept. of Labor was
created to serve the best interests of children.
The bureau did everything in its power to stimulate
community action for the welfare of children. One
of its stanchest allies was the library.

9.045   Lewis, George L. "Teaching Children to Use the
Library." Public Libraries 20 (1915):122-123.

What should be included in a session on
Bibliographic Instruction for an elementary school
class was completely outlined in this article.
Starting with a discussion of the concept of the
library, students were guided through an
understanding of its purpose and the composition of
its contents. The outline was an instructional tool
for the children's librarian to follow.

9.046   "Library Club Reports Growth of Reading Motivation
         Program." Publishers' Weekly 170 (1956):1968-1970.

         This was a report on the progress of the Library
         Club of America, Incorporated. Started by the Book
         Manufacturers' Institute, the goal was to stimulate
         reading among America's children. The work for the
         project was conducted in schools and libraries.

9.047   "Library Committee of the Junior Red Cross." School
         and Society 8 (1918):140-142.

         To address the aims of the Junior Red Cross, a
         library committee was established as an effective
         conduit to the young in the community. The
         objective of library service was to be a means of
         informing and recruiting children into the program
         of the Junior Red Cross.

9.048   Manchester, Elizabeth. "Relation of the Library to
         the Boy Scout and Camp Fire Girl Movement." Library
         Journal 39 (1914):752-760.

         Presented was the scheme for another approach to
         cooperation with units in the community, which
         served young people. To this end, the Detroit (MI)
         Public Library had designed a viable program for
         working, as well as supporting the Boy Scout and
         Camp Fire Girl movements.

9.049   Mandenhall, Ida M. "The School Library as a
         Laboratory." Wilson Library Bulletin 1 (1917):219-
         223.

         Developed was the concept of the school library
         serving as the laboratory of the educational
         experience. Inculcated in pupils should be a
         library syndrome, where their interests progressed
         from the school library to the public library for
         life.

9.050   Martin, Lowell. "Relation of Public and School
         Libraries in Serving Youth." ALA Bulletin 53
         (1959):112-117.

         There have been some differences between public and
         school libraries. However, the two agencies have a
         common goal. Both institutions are devoted to
         furthering the growth of children through reading,

which should provide a common ground for
cooperation.

9.051   Mathiews, F. K. "The Influence of the Boy Scout
          Movement in Directing the Reading of Boys." ALA
          Bulletin 8 (1914):223-228.

          Presented in this discussion were the various ways
          the Boy Scout Movement had developed to become an
          effective operative in the reading process. Through
          its handbook, Boy's Life Magazine, reading lists,
          and the Every Boy's Library, the movement was
          contributing sufficiently to the development of the
          reading habit in the lives of young males.

9.052   Mills, Forrest L. "Trends in Juvenile and Young
          Adult Use and Services." Library Quarterly 33
          (1963):58-69.

          Children and young adults were among the heaviest
          users of the public library. Part of the problem
          was the increase in school enrollment, the changes
          in the school curriculum and methods of teaching,
          and the weaknesses of the school library. These
          three factors explain the unprecedented use of
          public libraries by children and young adults.

9.053   Moore, Anne Carroll. "Library Visits to Public
          Schools." Library Journal 27 (1902):181-186.

          At the turn of the century, Brooklyn, New York was
          served by two separate public libraries, that of the
          Pratt Institute and its own municipal agency. How a
          cooperative program with area schools was developed
          and executed, was related by Anne Carroll Moore,
          then, the Children's Librarian for Pratt Institute
          Free Library.

9.054   National Educational Association. Report of
          Committee on the Relations of Public Libraries to
          Public Schools. Washington, DC: National
          Educational Association, 1899.

          In 1898, a Committee on Relations of Public
          Libraries to Public Schools was established by the
          National Educational Association. Its charge was to
          prepare lists of books which were suited for the
          reading and reference use of pupils in public
          schools, as well as to report on the relationship of
          the two agencies in the cooperative mode. Addressed

in this report was the need for early intervention
of both agencies into the development of the child.

9.055   Peckham, George W.   "The Child and the Book"
          Wisconsin Library Bulletin 2 (1906):90-93.

          Expanding the range of reading material to which a
          child could be exposed was one of the objectives of
          the Milwaukee (WI) Public Library. This was
          accomplished by a cooperative plan with the local
          school system.

9.056   Peckham, George W.   "Public Library and the Public
          Schools." Educational Review 8 (1894):358-362.

          Presented was a detailed account of the cooperative
          program, which had been devised by the Milwaukee
          (WI) Public Library to serve its local school
          system. The object of the project was to provide
          children with good books, especially for
          recreational purposes through their schools.

9.057   Peet, Harriet E.   "Co-operation Between Libraries
          and Schools - The Need in Chicago." Elementary
          School Teacher 6 (1906):310-317.

          From the perspective of the educator, a city's need
          for public library services was assessed. To
          cultivate the reading habit as a way of life, the
          Chicago school system could benefit from more branch
          libraries, classroom collections, story hours and
          reference services through its public library.

9.058   Power, Effie L.   "The Library in its Relation to the
          Elementary School." Public Libraries 11 (1906):544-
          548.

          It is the nature of instruction to be intensive,
          while the efforts of the library are extensive.
          When a pupil came to the library, he/she should be
          provided with an opportunity for reflective reading.
          Suggestions were forwarded on how such an objective
          could be achieved.

9.059   Power, Effie L.   "What the Public Libraries Can Do
          for Grade Schools." ALA Bulletin 10 (1916):215-216.

In elementary schools, the goal of library work
should be to effect an appreciation for good books,
as well as positive use of the public library. To
this end, a series of procedures were suggested by
public librarians to achieve this aim through direct
interaction with pupils and instructors.

9.060   Rathbone, Josephine A.   "Co-operation Between
Libraries and Schools: An Historical Sketch."
Library Journal 26 (1901):187-191.

Starting with 1876, the writer traced the evolution
of school/public library cooperation in the
professional arena. In the discussion were cited
the leading innovators on the national scene, ending
with the work of the Carnegie Library of Pittsburgh
(PA) and the Buffalo (NY) Public Library.

9.061   "Relations Between the Library and the Schools."
Special Libraries 11 (1920):97-98.

Coming from the announcement of the School
Department of the Newark (NJ) Public Library was a
list of the facets in school/library cooperation.
Outlined was how the library could aid the teacher,
as well as a listing of how the teacher could assist
the public library in the process of cooperation.

9.062   Rollins, Charlemae. "Children's Services Through
Community Organizations." Illinois Libraries 43
(1961):517-520.

Reaching children through adults can be accomplished
through community organizations. The organizations
to be tapped are churches, professional groups,
women's clubs, and the PTA.

9.063   Sanders, Minerva A.   "The Relation of the Public
Library to the School." Library Journal 14
(1889):79-83.

Two agents in the education of the young are the
public school and the public library. The public
library works side by side with the school.
Discussed is the program of the Pawtucket (RI)
Public Library.

9.064   Sanders, Minerva A. "Report on Reading for the
          Young." _Library_ _Journal_ 15 (1890):58-64.

          To make this report, the librarians were canvased to
          see what methods were used, what results were
          gleaned and what reading list had been created to
          foster the reading of the young. Attached to the
          report were sample replies from various public
          libraries.

9.065   Sargent, Mary. "Reading for the Young." _Library_
          Journal 14 (1889):226-236.

          Canvasing a variety of libraries, the 1889 report on
          reading for the young was made. School/library
          cooperation was still the dominate means of serving
          the young.

9.066   Sheehan, Ethna and A. Dorothy Perillo. "Selling a
          Library's Services." _Library_ _Journal_ 82 (1957):051-
          853.

          Using a political model, the Queens Borough (NY)
          Public Library found that it could sell a special
          program to teachers and parents. From a small
          beginning, the library displayed its services
          through exhibits, films and workshops to a larger
          audience.

9.067   Shelton, John L. "Project Uplift: Cultivating the
          Library Habit." _Wilson_ _Library_ _Bulletin_ 50
          (1975):59-62.

          When a program to recruit adults as new users to the
          library bombed, the focus of the program became the
          youth. In the Chattahoochee Valley and
          Kinchafooneek Regional Libraries (GA), the project
          coordinator decided on a scheme to indoctrinate the
          5th and 6th grades with the library habit.

9.068   Shortess, Lois F. "Cooperation Between Public and
          School Libraries." _Library_ _Journal_ 64 (1939):45-47.

          Many views surfaced on school/public library
          cooperation. In this article, the plea was being
          made for school libraries to serve as branches of
          the public library.

9.069   Smart, Lavila E.   "Visit to Public Library Brings
         Honor to Class." Library Journal 82 (1957):1336-
         1338.

         To encourage juvenile use of the Berkley (MI) Public
         Library, the library established an honor roll for
         grade school classes. Children could receive credit
         for their class if they came to the library to
         borrow books or to attend a group program. A
         certificate of merit was sent to the class; and it
         was announced in the local paper.

9.070   Smith, M. A. "Library Instruction in Schools."
         Wisconsin Library Bulletin 7 (1911):134-137.

         Over the years, many approaches were developed for
         orienting students to the public library. To
         accomplish this scheme of orientation, a combination
         of classroom and library visits were used with the
         librarian serving as facilitator of each.

9.071   Smith, Mary Allegra. "What the Librarian Needs from
         the Schools." Library Journal 37 (1912):169-174.

         According to this discussion, there were things that
         a librarian needed and had a right to expect in the
         area of cooperation from the educators. On the
         positive side librarians had made great efforts to
         cooperate with the schools. Grade schools were the
         place where cooperation must begin.

9.072   Taylor, Graham. "The Civic Value of Library Work
         with Children." ALA Bulletin (1908):380-381.

         Through the schools, playgrounds, and public
         libraries, children are introduced to democratic
         agencies where all were equally served. These
         agencies served as operatives for the nurturing of
         citizenship and the assimilation of the young into
         the American body politic.

9.073   Thompson, Laura A. "The Federal Children's Bureau."
         ALA Bulletin 8 (1914):215-218.

         By an Act of Congress in 1912 under the Department
         of Labor, the Children's Bureau was established.
         The purpose of the agency was to investigate the
         multitude of problems that impact on children on the
         social and economic scenes in American life. From

the work of this agency would come the use of the
birth certificate as a record for data gathering.

9.074   Van Buren, Maud. "Junior Civic League." Wisconsin
        Library Bulletin 6 (1910):133-136.

        Over the years, children's work pursued many types
        of programs to enhance the presence of the public
        library in the community. To such an end was
        developed the "Junior Civic League," which was a
        library sponsored project for civic pride that
        involved both males and females. How the Junior
        Civic League operated was the object of this
        discussion.

9.075   Wheeler, Joseph L.   "Home Reading with School
        Credit." Library Journal 45 (1920):679-682.

        As an example of interagency cooperation, this was a
        special project for grades 4 to 7, which was
        initiated by the Youngstown (OH) Public Library.
        Since the school mainly taught the mechanics of
        reading, the goals of the public library were to
        foster silent reading and to encourage the reading
        habit.

9.076   Wilkinson, Mary. "The St. Louis Playground Wagon."
        Library Journal 41 (1916):653-654.

        How to serve the city's playground was resolved with
        the design of a "playground wagon." Using the
        wagon, a collection of books was brought to the
        children; and during its stops stories were told.
        In detail, was presented the design of the vehicle
        used.

9.077   Wood, Harriet. "The Public Library and the School
        Library -A Joint Opportunity." Library Journal 45
        (1920):631-634.

        Whether in the school or the public library, the
        library should be perceived as an educational agent.
        Library orientation should begin in the first grade
        and should continue throughout the total educational
        experience. It should be conducted by both, the
        school and the public library.

10

Multi-Media

10.001   Anderson, Bert. "Cameraless Animation: How it Can
         Turn Kids On." Film Library Quarterly 6 (Winter,
         1972-73):27-30.

         Anderson discusses a workshop which was held for
         children's librarian, showing them how to have
         children make films.

10.002   Artel, Linda and Susan E. Wengraf. "Programming
         Children's Film." Film Library Quarterly 7:3 and 4
         (1974):50-60.

         Today's children are visually oriented from long
         hours in front of the television. Film programs
         will appeal to them. Presented are considerations
         for film programming in a library environment.

10.003   Barclay, Phyllis Langdon. "Film Selection for
         Children's Library Programs." Wilson Library
         Bulletin 29 (1955):378-80.

         The film is an art entirely of itself. There should
         be standards for good films for children. Films can
         be a part of a separate program or integrated into a
         general library hour, including films, stories and
         music.

10.004   Bough, Helen C. "The Children's Hour - With
         Stories, Films, and Records." Library Journal 82
         (1957):853-854.

         At the Chicago (IL) Public Library, the children's
         hour is an integrated program of stories, films and
         records. The objective of the program is to

heighten the appreciation of the various media for
children.

10.005   Bunting, Caroline Keen.   "Filming Young Readers for
         Globe-circling Picture.   Library Journal 76
         (1951):2105-2106+.

         At the New York (NY) Public Library, a film was
         produced recording a child's discovery of the world
         of books in an American public library.   The film
         was titled "The Republic of Childhood" and was
         produced by the State Department.

10.006   Fast, Elizabeth T.   "MEDIA: The Language of the
         Young."   Top of the New 33 (1976):50-63.

         Discussed is the value of media for children and
         young people.   The presentation is divided by such
         categories as 1) media as a mode of presentation; 2)
         media as part of the circulating collection; 3)
         media as a source of reference information; 4) media
         as a means of creative expression by patrons; 5)
         media literacy.   The discussion focuses on the
         school use and the application by the public
         library.

10.007   Faulkner, Nancy.   "TV - Bridge to Reading."   Library
         Journal 77 (1952):1461-1463.

         In Seattle, WA, there was a program called
         "Teladventure Tales."   The purpose of the program
         was to stimulate the reading interest of children
         six to sixteen via the television.

10.008   Filstrup, Janie.   "Children and Picture Blocks -
         Story Making and Telling."   Top of the News 29
         (1972):46-53.

         Letter blocks have been a staple of childhood for
         ages.   Making picture blocks was a play on an old
         theme, which would be used with children for
         storytelling.   The "how" of the process was
         presented in this article.

10.009   Geiser, Cynthia.   "Selecting and Using Story
         Recordings."   Library Journal 85 (1960):4521-4523.
         When selecting story records for children, choose
         only the best.   To this end, criteria for selection

is presented herein. Presented are the objectives
for use of records with the young.

10.010   Jinnette, Isabella. "TV Story Program." Library
Journal 78 (1953):981-983.

On a experimental basis, the Enoch Pratt Free
Library of Baltimore, Maryland conducted a TV story
hour, which was called, "Step into Storyland." The
program was fifteen minutes in length and was
designed for children 5 - 9 years of age.
Throughout the library system, there were signs of
the success of the program.

10.011   Johnson, Jean. "Children's TV: The Challenge to
ACT." Top of the News 32 (1976):65-72.

Action for Children's Television (ACT) serves as a
monitor of children's programming on television.
"Since its formation in 1968, ACT has been
responsible for revisions in advertising policies
concerning children and has significantly altered
the climate of decision making in which network
executives formulate children's programming
practices."

10.012   Knauer, Kay. "Tell it Again - In Many Ways: Mead
Uses Puppets, Cut-outs, Flannel, Drawings, Dolls."
Wisconsin Library Bulletin 72 (1976):163-164.

Telling a story over and over appeals to young
children. Stories can be told, then done with
creative dramatics, using puppets, dolls or with a
flannel graph.

10.013   Le Clercq, Anne. "Featuring Films: A Children's
Librarian's Programmatic View." School Library
Journal 18 (1972):39-40.

Using films with the public is a valid service of
the public library. The range of feature films for
children is wide and varied, as well as will capture
their attention.

10.014   Mannon-Tissot, Thalia. "Innovation Through Trial
and Error." Film Library Quarterly 2 (Fall,
1969):13-15.

At the Brooklyn (NY) Public Library, a children's
librarian explains her experimentation with film
programs for children.

10.015   Miller, Marlyn M.   "The Application of Audio-Visual
         Aids in Library Pre-school Storyhours."   MA Thesis,
         Kent State University, 1954.

         The object of this study was to assess the
         incorporation of audio-visual aids in the pre-school
         story hour.   Records were the most widely used item.

10.016   Mohr, Nelda and Thalia Mannon-Tissot.   "Cents and
         Non-Cents of AV Crafts."   Top of the News 28
         (1972):173-178.

         Providing ideas on the basics of AV crafts, this
         article could serve as a guide.   Starting with zero
         funds, a children's librarian could make such
         projects as slides and film with children.

10.017   Moll, Joy K. and Patricia Hermann.   "Evaluation and
         Selection of Toys, Games, and Puzzles: Manipulative
         Materials in Library Collections."   Top of the News
         31 (1974):86-89.

         Acknowledging that youth learn and retain
         information in different ways, educational agencies
         are adding toys, games and puzzles to their library
         collections for children.   Manipulative materials
         require a different set of criteria for evaluation
         and selection; the points of focus are presented in
         this article.

10.018   Pellowski, Anne.   "Children's Cinema: International
         Dilemma or Delight?"   Film Library Quarterly 2
         (Fall, 1969):5-11.

         Whatever the form, the goal of the children's
         librarian is to bring children opportunities for
         exposure to imaginative, entertaining,
         mindstretching and revealing expressions of the
         human mind.   Through film, this is accomplished.
         Attached is a bibliography of resources on using
         films with children.

10.019   Peterson, Carolyn Sue.   "Practically Speaking."
         School Library Journal 21 (1975):26-27.

         Training different personnel of community agencies
         to share literature with children is a project of
         the Orlando (FL) Public Library.   Through workshop
         sessions, adults and young people are taught to use
         puppetry, flannel boards and other media with
         children.

10.020   Plummer, Julia.   "A Children's Librarian Views the
         Future."   ALA Bulletin 29 (1935):698-700.

         Stating that for forty years, children's librarians
         had been dependent on book collections to stimulate
         juvenile interest in reading, now was the time of
         the radio, motion pictures, and the motorcar.   By
         tying into the radio and movie, the library could
         expand its contact with the young.

10.021   Poignand, John and Peggy Mann.   "Curtain of Illusion
         - The Odyssey of the Children's Caravan."   School
         Library Journal 13 (1967):46-49.

         Morton Schindel of Weston Woods Studios created
         mobile vans to take films and books to juvenile
         special populations.   Isolated populations were
         served in New Jersey, northern Michigan, and
         Appalachia through a grant from the Office of
         Economic Opportunity.

10.022   Rathbun, Norma L.   "Tel-adventure Time-TV Brings
         Child and Book Together."   ALA Bulletin 46
         (1952):143-145.

         Librarians were finding that television served as an
         affective medium for bringing children and books
         together.   A growing number of libraries were
         producing TV story hours.

10.023   Ross, Eulalie Steinmetz.   "Hints from a TV
         Storyteller."   Library Journal 81 (1956):981-984.

         Ross related her experiences with a television story
         hour for the Cincinnati (OH) Public Library.
         Programming was done for children six to twelve.
         For each program five to six boys and girls were
         invited from a branch library to be apart of a live
         audience.

10.024   Schindel, Morton. "The Picture Book Projected."
         School Library Journal 14 (1968):46-47.

         For the young child, the most enjoyable encounter
         comes with a picture book. Schindel wanted
         professionals to share this joy of picture books to
         large groups; thus to this end, he developed the
         reproduction of picture books as filmstrips.

10.025   "Sesame Street - What Next?" School Library Journal
         17 (1970):22-25.

         Moving into its second season, libraries reviewed
         their tie-ins to Seasame Street. Appointed was a
         reading reinforcement committee to review and select
         titles of books to be used with the Sesame Street
         program.

10.026   Shannon, Linda. "The Preschool Adventure Library."
         School Library Journal 22 (1975):25-27.

         The Preschool Adventure Library is a service of the
         Cambria County (Johnstown, PA) Library System.
         Through PAL, the preschooler encounters multi-media
         that allows him/her to learn through direct
         experience.

10.027   Shaw, Spencer G. "Children's Records: An
         Evaluative Appraisal." Library Journal 80
         (1955):2316-2323.

         The growing number of records for children should
         receive the same review attention that is accorded
         books. Special consideration should be given to the
         Play or Activity Record and the Story Record.
         Presented herein are some standard points for
         reviewing this medium.

10.028   Shaw, Spencer. "Records Can Teach Values." Library
         Journal 73 (1948):1484-1487.

         Integrating records into story hours and book talks
         was a positive method of conveying values to young
         audiences. Contained in this article are the
         guidelines for the use of recordings, along with
         some suggested programming.

10.029   Shayon, Robert Lewis. "Television and Children's
         Reading." Horn Book 29 (1953):91-100.

         Man thought that the written word would always be
         the only method of learning. Then, there appeared
         the television, which captured the interest of the
         young, which could be used to enhance their reading.

10.030   Shea, Agatha. "Radio as a Feature of Children's
         Work in The Chicago Public Library." Illinois
         Libraries 13 (1931):142-144.

         For two years, the Chicago Public Library had
         conducted the Radio Book Club. Through the program,
         children were introduced to the library and a host
         of books.

10.031   Sivulich, Kenneth G. and Sandra Stroner Sivulich.
         "Media Library for Preschoolers: A Service of the
         Erie (PA) Metropolitan Library." Top of the News 31
         (1974):49-54.

         Providing the right materials to the right patron,
         took on new meaning at the Erie (PA) Metropolitan
         Library. For preschoolers, the library provided
         books, filmstrips, movies, games, puzzles, and pets
         in a special Media Library.

10.032   Snook, Vera J. "Getting Films for Small Children."
         Library Journal 44 (1919):157-158.

         For six years, the Reddick's Library of Ottawa, IL
         had had film programs for children. Featured were
         presentations of fairy tales, comedies, war and
         patriotic matter, dramatizations of stories and
         events, as well as travel and industrial movies.

10.033   Steinmetz, Eulalie. "Storytelling versus
         Recordings." Horn Book 24 (1948):163-172.

         Should records be used to convey stories in story
         hour? According to this librarian, records did not
         allow for the interplay between the teller and the
         audience and should not be used.

10.034   Thompson, Daphne. "Curious George in the Tomato
         Field: Regional Library Service to Migrant
         Children." Top of the News 30 (1974):420-424.

To serve the children of migrant workers, the
Eastern Shore Area Library (MD) rented a Children's
Caravan mediamobile from Weston Woods. Working in
four counties, the mobile and staff took movies,
puppet shows, filmstrips, music, and books to this
special population.

10.035   "Toys and Games - 'The First Reading Tool.'" School
         Library Journal 21 (1975):24-27.

         This was an interview with Edythe O. Cawthorne, the
         Coordinator of Children's Services for Prince
         George's County (MD) Memorial System. Under
         Cawthorne's guidance the system started lending toys
         and games to their young clients.

10.036   Weisblat, Genevieve and John. "The Exciting
         Adventure of the Children's Caravan." Top of the
         News 23 (1967):158-164.

         Working in the Bridgeton, NJ area and surrounding
         environment, the children's caravan took multimedia
         programs to the children of migrant workers. Not
         only did the programs appeal to children, but the
         adults, as well, who were appreciative of the
         exposure to library materials.

10.037   Young, Diana. "People, Puppets, and You." Top of
         the News 31 (1975):218-219.

         Puppets capture the imagination of all children and
         are an excellent drawing card for libraries.
         Children's librarians can use their favorite stories
         or write scripts of their own for puppet shows. In
         communities, there are puppeteers who will volunteer
         their time for a program.

Author Index

Subject Index

[Numbers are entry numbers, not page numbers]

A

Action for Children's
  Television (ACT), 10.011
Adams, Charles Francis,
  9.011
Administration, 1.005,
  3.009, 3.014, 3.019,
  3.029, 3.030, 4.079, 4.081
Adolescence, see youth
Adults, 5.021, 8.033
Age limits, 7.083
Albany (NY) Public Library,
  7.072
Alley Library (DC), 7.029
Americanization, 4.073,
  5.029, 7.082
Animal Protective League,
  7.004
Audio-visual aids, see media

B

Baker, Augusta, 2.004
Bell, Thelma, 7.084
Berkley (MI) Public Library,
  9.069
Bibliotherapy, 5.028
Bilingual Program, 8.085,
  8.093
Bingham Library for Youth,
  1.025
Birtwell, Charles Wesley,
  1.017
Black children, 4.106,
  5.018, 7.001, 7.002,

7.089, 8.045
Black librarians, 2.004,
  2.060, 2.063
Blind children, 8.090
Book Club, 7.053
Book Lists, 7.015
Book Magic Hour, 7.055
Book Reviews, 6.010, 6.035
Book Selection, 6.002,
  6.003, 6.005, 6.006,
  6.011, 6.014, 6.015,
  6.024, 6.025, 6.027,
  6.028, 6.030, 6.033,
  6.034, 6.035, 6.036, 6.037
Book Talks, 7.036
Books, 4.025, 4.071, 4.097,
  4.104, 5.026, 5.027, 6.029
Bookshop for Boys and Girls,
  4.074
Book Week, 1.004, 1.030,
  7.043, 9.014
Boston (MA) Public Library,
  1.011, 1.015, 7.032,
  8.044, 9.013
Boy's Club, 9.002
Bridgeton, NJ, 10.036
Brooklyn (NY) Public
  Library, 7.074, 7.082,
  8.014, 8.023, 10.014
Buffalo (NY) Library, 3.004,
  9.026, 9.060

C

California, 1.031; Palo
  Alto, 3.026; Pasadena,

About the Compiler

FANNETTE H. THOMAS is Public Services Librarian at Essex Community College Library in Baltimore County, Maryland. This is her first book.